Contents

P9-CAL-604

Consonants

Theme: My Favorite Things

Unit Opener: Read Aloud, poem "In My Tree House" by J. Patrick Lewis . . .5

Home Letter 6

Partner Letters 7–8

Consonants s, t, b

The sound of s: Phonemic awareness/ Sound to symbol 9–10

The sound of t: Phonemic awareness/ Sound to symbol 11–12

The sound of b: Phonemic awareness/ Sound to symbol 13–14

Initial/final consonants s, t, b 15–16

Consonants h, m, k

The sound of h: Phonemic awareness/ Sound to symbol 17–18

The sound of m: Phonemic awareness/ Sound to symbol 19–20

The sound of k: Phonemic awareness/ Sound to symbol 21–22

Initial/final consonants h, m, k 23–24

Consonants j, f, g

The sound of j: Phonemic awareness/ Sound to symbol 25–26

The sound of f: Phonemic awareness/ Sound to symbol 27–28

The sound of g: Phonemic awareness/ Sound to symbol 29–30

Initial/final consonants j, f, g 31–32

Consonants l, d, n

The sound of l: Phonemic awareness/ Sound to symbol 33–34

The sound of d: Phonemic awareness/ Sound to symbol 35–36

The sound of n: Phonemic awareness/ Sound to symbol 37–38

Initial/final consonants l, d, n 39–40

Consonants w, c, r, p, q, v

The sound of w: Phonemic awareness/ Sound to symbol 41–42

The sound of c: Phonemic awareness/ Sound to symbol 43–44

The sound of r: Phonemic awareness/ Sound to symbol 45–46

The sound of p: Phonemic awareness/ Sound to symbol 47–48

The sound of qu: Sound to symbol 49

The sound of v: Sound to symbol 50

Initial/final consonants w, c, r, p, q, v . . .51–52

Consonants x, y, z

The sound of x: Sound to symbol 53

The sound of y: Sound to symbol 54

The sound of z: Sound to symbol 55

Initial/final consonants x, y, z 56

Medial consonants 57–58

Review consonants: Phonics & Spelling 59

Phonics & Writing: A Sentence 60

Take-Home Book: "Camping Fun" 61–62

Unit Checkup: Consonants 63–64

Short Vowels

Theme: Amazing Animals

Unit Opener: Read Aloud, "Frogs Call" . . .65

Home Letter .66

Short Vowel a

Phonemic awareness/ Phonograms, rhyme 67–68

Sound to symbol 69–70

Blending 71–72

Spelling/Words in context 73–74

Spelling/Words in context 75–76

Review short vowel a: Phonics & Reading . .77

Phonics & Writing: Building Words 78
Take-Home Book: "Bats" 79–80
High-frequency words 81–82

Short Vowel i

Phonemic awareness/
Phonograms, rhyme 83–84
Sound to symbol 85–86
Short Vowels a, i: Blending 87–88
Spelling/Words in context 89–90
Spelling/Words in context 91–92
Review short i: Phonics & Reading 93
Phonics & Writing: Building Words 94
Take-Home Book: "Fast Pig" 95–96
High-frequency words 97–98

Short Vowel u

Phonemic awareness/
Phonograms, rhyme 99–100
Sound to symbol 101–102
Short vowels a, i, u:
Blending 103–104
Spelling/Words in context 105–106
Spelling/Words in context 107–108
Review short u: Phonics & Reading 109
Phonics & Writing: Building Words 110
Take-Home Book: "Lunch in a Jug" . . 111–112

Short Vowel o

Phonemic awareness/
Phonograms, rhyme 113–114
Sound to symbol 115–116
Short vowels a, i, u, o:
Blending 117–118
Spelling/Words in context 119–120
Spelling/Words in context 121–122
Review short o: Phonics & Reading 123
Phonics & Writing: Building Words 124
Take-Home Book: "In the Tub" 125–126
High-frequency words 127–128

Short Vowel e

Phonemic awareness/
Phonograms, rhyme 129–130
Sound to symbol 131
Picture-Text Match 132
Short vowels a, i, o, u, e:
Blending 133–134
Spelling/Words in context 135–136
Spelling/Words in context 137-138
Review short vowels: Phonics & Spelling . . 139
Phonics & Writing: A Postcard 140
Take-Home Book: "Fish Food" 141–142
Unit Checkup: Short vowels,
High-frequency words 143–144

Long Vowels

UNIT 3

Theme: Let's Play

Unit Opener: Read Aloud, poem
"Play" by Frank Asch 145
Home Letter 146

Long Vowel a

Phonemic awareness/
Phonograms, rhyme 147–148
Sound to symbol 149–150
Long and short vowel a:
Phonemic awareness 151
Long vowel a: Sound to symbol 152
Sound to symbol/Rhyming 153–154
Spelling/Words in context 155–156

Spelling/Words in context 157–158
Review long vowel a: Phonics & Reading . . 159
Phonics & Writing: Building Words 160
Take-Home Book: "Make a Face" . . . 161–162
High-frequency words 163–164

Long Vowel i

Phonemic awareness/
Phonograms, rhyme 165–166
Sound to symbol 167–168
Long and short vowel i:
Phonemic awareness 169
Long and short vowels a, i: Sound to symbol 170

Spelling/ Words in context **171–172**

Spelling/ Words in context **173–174**

Review long vowel i:
   Phonics & Reading **175**

Phonics & Writing: Building Words **176**

Take-Home Book: "Di Tries" **177–178**

High-frequency words **179–180**

Long vowel u

Phonemic awareness/
   Phonograms, rhyme **181–182**

Sound to symbol **183–184**

Long and short vowel u:
   Phonemic awareness **185**

Long vowel u: Phonemic awareness **186**

Sound to symbol/Words in context . . . **187–188**

Spelling: Words in context **189–190**

Long and short vowels a, i, u: Spelling **191**

Review long vowels a, i, u:
   Phonemic awareness **192**

Review long vowel u:
   Phonics & Reading **193**

Phonics & Writing: Building Words **194**

Take-Home Book: "Hand Games" . . . **195–196**

Long Vowel o

Phonemic awareness/
   Sound to symbol **197–198**

Phonograms/Sound to symbol **199–200**

Spelling/Reading **201–202**

Long and short vowel o: Phonemic
   awareness/Sound to symbol **203–204**

Sound to symbol/
   Words in context **205–206**

Spelling/Words in context **207–208**

Spelling **209**

Review long vowels a, i, u, o:
   Sound to symbol **210**

Phonics & Reading **211**

Phonics & Writing: Building Words **212**

Take-Home Book: "Games Around
   the Globe" **213–214**

High-frequency words **215–216**

Long Vowel e

Phonemic awareness/
   Phonograms, rhyme **217–218**

Sound to symbol/
   Phonemic awareness **219–220**

Long and short vowels a, i, e:
   Phonemic awareness **221**

Long vowel e: Phonograms, rhyme **222**

Sound to symbol/Words in context . . . **223–224**

Spelling/Words in context **225–226**

Spelling **227**

Review long vowels a, i, u, o, e:
   Phonemic awareness **228**

Review long and short a, i, u, o, e:
   Blending **229–230**

Review long vowels: Spelling **231**

Review long and short vowels: Spelling . . . **232**

Review long vowels: Phonics & Spelling . . . **233**

Phonics & Writing: A Friendly Letter **234**

Take-Home Book: "No Sleep" **235–236**

Unit Checkup: Long vowels,
   High-frequency words **237–238**

Consonant Blends, Y as a Vowel

UNIT 4

Theme: Everybody Eats

Unit Opener: Read Aloud,
   "Everybody Eats Bread" **239**

Home Letter **240**

R blends: Sound to symbol **241–242**

R blends: Sound to symbol/Spelling . **243–244**

L blends: Sound to symbol **245–246**

L blends: Spelling/Words in context . . **247–248**

S blends: Sound to symbol **249–250**

S blends: Spelling/Words in context . . **251–252**

Final blends:
   Sound to symbol/Spelling **253–254**

Review Initial/Final blends:
   Blending **255–256**

Review consonant blends:
Phonics & Reading 257

Phonics & Writing: Building Words 258

Y as a vowel: Sound to symbol 259–260

Y as a vowel:
Words in Context/Spelling 261–262

Review consonant blends and y as a vowel:
Spelling 263

Phonics & Writing: A Shopping List 264

Take-Home Book: "Pizza Feast" 265–266

Unit Checkup: Consonant blends,
Y as a vowel 267–268

 UNIT 5

Endings, Digraphs, Contractions
Theme: Whatever the Weather

Unit Opener: Read Aloud,
"Let it Snow!" 269

Home Letter 270

Inflectional endings –ed and –ing/
Base words 271–272

Inflectional endings –ed and –ing:
Words in context 273–274

Consonant digraph th:
Phonemic awareness 275

Discriminating between th and t:
Spelling 276

Consonant digraph wh:
Phonemic awareness 277

Wh and th: Spelling 278

Consonant digraph sh:
Phonemic awareness 279

Discriminating between sh and s:
Spelling 280

Consonant digraph ch:
Phonemic awareness 281

Ch and c: Spelling 282

Consonant digraph kn:
Spelling/Words in context 283–284

Review Consonant digraphs:
Words in context 285–286

Consonant digraphs: Blending 287

Review consonant digraphs: Reading 288

Review endings, digraphs:
Phonics & Reading 289

Phonics & Writing: Building Words 290

Take-Home Book: "Clouds" 291–292

Contractions with will:
Words in context 293

Contractions with is:
Words in context 294

Contractions with am and are:
Words in context 295

Contractions with not:
Words in context 296

Review contractions:
Words in context 297–298

Review endings, consonant digraphs,
contractions: Phonics & Spelling 299

Phonics & Writing:
A Description 300

Take-Home Book: "It's Raining" 301–302

Unit Checkup: Endings, digraphs,
contractions 303–304

In My Tree House
by J. Patrick Lewis

Up in my tree house,
Spring's on parade,
And we've got two cool, leafy
Seats in the shade.

If you eat an apple,
I'll eat one too,
And we'll sit in my tree house,
Enjoying the view.

What is your favorite place to be?

HOME LETTER

Dear Family,

In this unit about "My Favorite Things," your child will be learning about consonants and the sounds they make. Many of your child's favorite things begin with consonants, such as home, pets, music, fun, and books. As your child becomes familiar with consonant sounds, you might try these activities together.

▶ Help your child make a Letter Book. Your child can print a letter on each page, then tape or glue on pictures that begin with that letter.

▶ Read the poem on page 5 aloud. Help your child to identify the consonants at the beginning of words such as house and view.

▶ Your child might enjoy reading these books with you. Look for them in your local library.

The Very Hungry Caterpillar by Eric Carle

A Pocket for Corduroy by Don Freeman

Sincerely,

_____

Estimada familia:

En esta unidad, titulada "Mis cosas favoritas" ("My Favorite Things"), su hijo/a estudiará las consonantes y sus sonidos. Muchas de las cosas favoritas de su hijo/a comienzan con consonantes, como home (juegos), pets (mascotas), music (música), fun (diversión) y books (libros). A medida que su hijo/a se vaya familiarizando con los sonidos de las consonantes, pueden hacer las siguientes actividades juntos.

▶ Ayuden a su hijo/a a hacer un Libro de letras. Su hijo/a puede escribir una letra en cada página y después unir con cinta adhesiva o pegamento dibujos que comiencen con esa letra.

▶ Lean en voz alta el poema en la página 5. Ayuden a su hijo/a a identificar las consonantes al principio de palabras como house (casa) y view (vista).

▶ Ustedes y su hijo/a disfrutarán leyendo estos libros juntos. Búsquenlos en su biblioteca local.

The Very Hungry Caterpillar de Eric Carle

A Pocket for Corduroy de Don Freeman

Sinceramente,

_____

Name _____

Bb go together.
Bb are partner letters.

Color **each ball that has partner letters on it.**

Look at the letter above each picture. Circle each word that begins with its partner letter.

1. F — fox, card, fan, meat, fish

2. d — Dave, Sam, Don, Dina, Mary

3. H — home, boat, hill, king, hook

4. k — Ken, Kyle, Tara, Kurt, Matt

5. M — nose, monkey, hand, milk, mask

6. t — Tom, Tyler, Tina, Mia, Jake

7. P — dish, pig, peel, top, pen

8. r — Rosa, Ryan, Bobby, Katie, Ross

9. w — Wendy, Helen, Will, Wyatt, Sarah

Ask your child to write his or her name, then write partner letters for each consonant.

Name_____

Suzy sat on the sand.
Suzy sat by the sea.
Suzy sat in the sun.
Suzy sat with me.

▶ **Sand begins with the sound of s.** Circle **each picture whose name begins with the sound of s.**

1.	2.	3.	4.
5.	6.	7.	8.
9.	10.	11.	12.

The sound of s: Phonemic awareness   **9**

Say the name of each picture. If it begins with the sound of **s**, print **s** on the line. Then trace the whole word.

1.

aw

2.

ent

3.

un

4.

ix

5.

oll

6.

ock

7.

uit

8.

at

9.

ail

10.

orse

11.

ink

12.

eat

The sound of s: Sound to symbol

HOME

Say, "Sister Sue sells _____." Ask your child to finish the sentence with words that begin with s.

Name_____

Ten toy tigers
Sat down for tea.
Ten tails tipped the table—
Oh, dear me!

> Tea **begins with the sound of t.** Circle **each picture whose name begins with the sound of t.**

1.
2.
3.
4.
5.
6.
7.
8.
9.
10.
11.
12.

The sound of t: Phonemic awareness   **11**

Say the name of each picture. If it begins with the sound of **t**, print **t** on the line. Then trace the whole word.

1.

op

2.

ire

3.

aw

4.

ent

5.

ape

6.

ed

7.

en

8.

ack

9.

ub

10.

ose

11.

oys

12.

un

 HOME

Ask your child to name three objects in your home that begin with the sound of *t*.

Name_____

Let's bounce the ball high,
Let's bounce the ball low.
Let's bounce the ball fast,
Let's bounce the ball slow.

> Ball **begins with the sound of b.** Circle **each picture whose name begins with the sound of b.**

1.	2.	3.	4.
5.	6.	7.	8.
9.	10.	11.	12.

The sound of b: Phonemic awareness   **13**

Say the name of each picture. If it begins with the sound of **b**, print **b** on the line. Then trace the whole word.

1.

ag

2.

oat

3.

all

4.

elt

5.

ock

6.

ox

7.

at

8.

un

9.

us

10.

ed

11.

oys

12.

ug

Say "Buddy bought a ___." Ask your child to add a word that begins with the sound of *b*.

Name _____

> Say the name of each picture. If the name **begins** with the sound of the letter in the box, print it on the first line. If it **ends** with that sound, print it on the second line.

1. **b**

b

2. **t**

3. **s**

4. **b**

5. **t**

6. **b**

7. **s**

8. **b**

9. **b**

10. **s**

11. **t**

12. **s**

▶ Say **each picture name.** Draw **a line through the pictures in a row that begin with the same letter sound.** Write **the letter that wins in each game.**

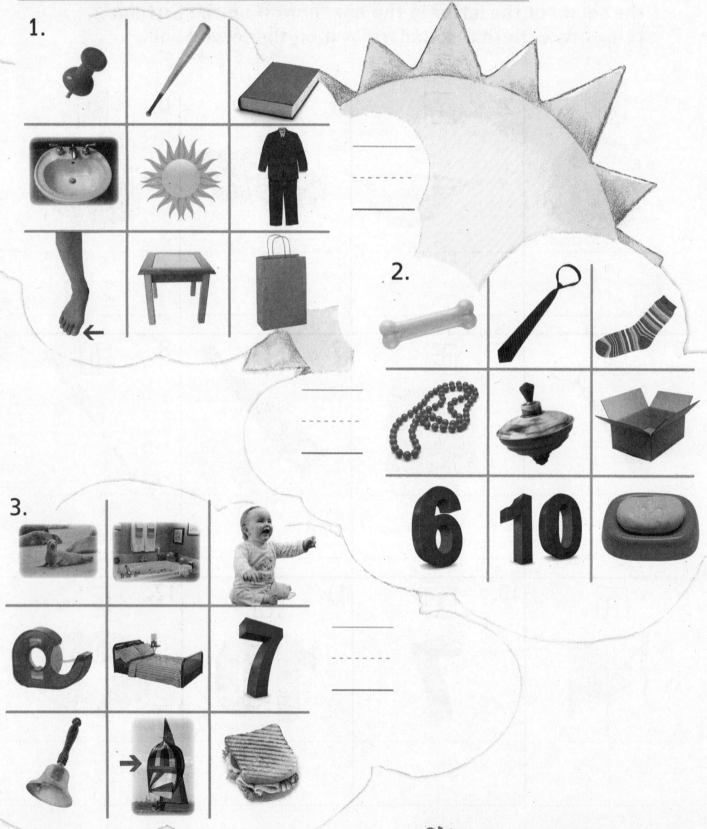

1.

2.

3.

16   **Initial consonants s, t, b**

Name_____

My hamster has been running
On his wheel since half past five.
He's gone a hundred miles by now,
So when will he arrive?

> Hamster **begins with the sound of h.** Say **the name of each picture.** Circle **the beginning letter of the picture name. Then** circle **each picture whose name begins with the sound of h.**

1.
S
T
B
(H)

2.
T
B
H
S

3.
B
H
S
T

4.
S
H
T
B

5.
B
T
H
S

6.
T
H
S
B

The sound of h: Phonemic awareness   **17**

Say the name of each picture. If it begins with the sound of **h**, print **h** on the line. Then trace the whole word.

1.

_____ at

2.

_____ an

3.

_____ eart

4.

_____ ot

5.

_____ am

6.

_____ op

7.

_____ and

8.

_____ ill

9.

_____ ose

10.

_____ ey

11.

_____ eel

12.

_____ en

 HOME

Point to the picture of the hen. Ask your child to think of other animals whose names begin with h.

Name _____

Mom gave me a muffin for lunch.
Mom gave me a muffin to munch.
The muffin I munched was yummy.
The muffin is in my tummy.

> Mom **begins with the sound of m.** Circle **each**
> picture whose name begins with the sound of **m.**

1.

2.

3.

4.

5.

6.

7.

8.

9.

10.

11.

12.

Say the name of each picture. If it begins with the sound of **m**, print **m** on the line. Then trace the whole word.

1. _____ oon

2. _____ op

3. _____ ask

4. _____ all

5. _____ ix

6. _____ an

7. _____ ouse

8. _____ ap

9. _____ ilk

10. _____ op

11. _____ eart

12. _____ eat

The sound of m: Sound to symbol

Point to a picture. Have your child say its name and then think of a word that begins with the same sound.

Name _____

Where's Katy's kite?
Where's Katy's key?
Where's Katy's kitty?
Katy has lost all three!

Kite **begins with the sound of k.** Say **the name of each** picture. Circle **the beginning letter of the picture name. Then** circle **each picture whose name begins with the sound of k.**

1.
H
M
K
T

2.
M
K
T
H

3.
K
T
H
M

4.
T
K
M
H

5.
H
M
K
T

6.
T
H
M
K

Say the name of each picture. If it begins with the sound of **k**, print **k** on the line. Then trace the whole word.

1. \
ey

2. \
ike

3. \
ing

4. \
ook

5. \
ite

6. \
ork

7. \
ilk

8. \
itten

9. \
itchen

10. \
etchup

The sound of k: Sound to symbol

 Taking turns with your child, think of more words that begin with the sound of k, such as *keep* and *kind*.

Name _____

Say the name of each picture. Find the beginning letter of each picture name. Circle that letter.

1.

H M K

2.

M K H

3.

K H M

4.

H M K

5.

K M H

6.

M H K

7.

H K M

8.

K M H

9.

M H K

10.

H K M

11.

K M H

12.

M H K

Say the name of each picture. If the name **begins** with the sound of the letter in the box, print it on the first line. If it **ends** with that sound, print it on the second line.

1. | k |

_____

k

2. | h |

_____

3. | m |

_____

4. | m |

_____

5. | k |

_____

6. | m |

_____

7. | k |

_____

8. | h |

_____

9. | h |

_____

10. | k |

_____

11. | m |

_____

12. | k |

_____

 HOME Ask your child to name two pictures that begin with the same sound and two that end with the same sound.

Name _____

Joy can pick a prize.
It will be hers to keep.
Will she take the jacks or the jet,
The jump rope or the jeep?

▶ **Jeep** **begins with the sound of j.** Circle **each picture whose name begins with the sound of j.**

1.

2.

3.

4.

5.

6.

7.

8.

9.

Say the name of each picture. If it begins with the sound of j, print j on the line. Then trace the whole word.

1.

eep

2.

eaf

3.

ug

4.

ent

5.

eel

6.

ump

7.

et

8.

ouse

9.

un

10.

ug

11.

ack

12.

ar

Help your child think of sentences using words that begin with *j*, such as *Joe juggled the jacks*.

Name _____

Five furry foxes
Fanning in the heat.
They all run away
On furry fox feet.

▶ **Five begins with the sound of f. Circle each picture whose name begins with the sound of f.**

1.

2.

3.

4.

5.

6.

7.

8.

9.

10.

11.

12.

Say the name of each picture. If it begins with the sound of **f**, print **f** on the line. Then trace the whole word.

1.

ish

2.

eaf

3.

our

4.

eet

5.

ive

6.

an

7.

ail

8.

ork

9.

ence

10.

amp

11.

ox

12.

ire

Make up riddles for your child to answer with words from the page, such as *What rhymes with box?* (*fox*)

Name_____

Get the gifts.
Do not be late.
Run to the garden,
And open the gate.

> Garden **begins with the sound of g.** Circle **each picture whose name begins with the sound of g.**

1.

2.

3.

4.

5.

6.

7.

8.

9.

The sound of g: Phonemic awareness   **29**

Say **the name of each picture. If it begins with the sound of g,** print **g on the line. Then** trace **the whole word.**

1.

_____ um

2.

_____ irl

3.

_____ ive

4.

_____ old

5.

_____ ame

6.

_____ og

7.

_____ ate

8.

_____ ift

9.

_____ oat

10.

_____ ag

11.

_____ ig

12.

_____ oose

The sound of g: Sound to symbol

Invite your child to think of more words that begin with g such as *go, get, good, give.*

Name_____

> Say the name of each picture. If the name **begins** with the sound of the letter in the box, print it on the first line. If it **ends** with that sound, print it on the second line.

1. **f**

_____ | _____

2. **j**

_____ | _____

3. **g**

_____ | _____

4. **f**

_____ | _____

5. **g**

_____ | _____

6. **f**

_____ | _____

7. **f**

_____ | _____

8. **j**

_____ | _____

9. **g**

_____ | _____

10. **j**

_____ | _____

11. **g**

_____ | _____

12. **f**

_____ | _____

▶ **Say the name of each toy. Print a letter to finish the word on each sign. Then trace the word.**

1. et

2. ish

3. oat

4. bu

5. do

6. ame

7. eep

8. arm

32 Initial/final consonants j, f, g

Ask your child to finish sentences using words from the page, such as *Cows and ducks live on a _____. (farm)*

Name_____

Look, look, Lizzy!
Quick, come and see.
A lovely little ladybug
Just landed on me.

> Ladybug **begins with the sound of l.** Circle **each picture whose name begins with the sound of l.**

1.

2.

3.

4.

5.

6.

7.

8.

9.

10.

11.

12.

Say the name of each picture. If it begins with the sound of **l**, print **l** on the line. Then trace the whole word.

1.

og

2.

ell

3.

ock

4.

ill

5.

ips

6.

eaf

7.

amp

8.

oll

9.

ake

10.

all

11.

id

12.

etter

34   The sound of l: Sound to symbol

 Ask your child to use two of the *l* words in a sentence, such as *I saw a log in the lake.*

Name _____

Denny does the dishes.
Dori does them, too.
Dad feeds the dog,
And soon they are through.

> Dishes **begins with the sound of d. Circle each picture whose name begins with the sound of d.**

1.

2.

3.

4.

5.

6.

7.

8.

9.

10.

11.

12.

Say the name of each picture. If it begins with the sound of **d**, print **d** on the line. Then trace the whole word.

1.

_ _ oll

2.

_ _ oot

3.

_ _ oor

4.

_ _ id

5.

_ _ ey

6.

_ _ uck

7.

_ _ ive

8.

_ _ eer

9.

_ _ og

10.

_ _ esk

11.

_ _ ishes

12.

_ _ arn

Ask your child to name three objects in your home that begin with the *d* sound.

Name _____

No, no, Nellie.
No, no, Ned.
Do not jump up
On my nice neat bed.

▶ **No** begins with the sound of **n**. **Circle** each picture whose name begins with the sound of **n**.

1.

2.

3.

4.

5. →

6.

7.

8.

9.

10.

11.

12.

The sound of n: Phonemic awareness   **37**

Say the name of each picture. If it begins with the sound of n, print n on the line. Then trace the whole word.

1.

‗est

2.

10

‗en

3.

‗ose

4.

‗ut

5.

‗us

6.

9

‗ine

7.

‗aby

8.

‗an

9.

‗urse

10.

‗op

11.

‗et

12.

‗ail

 With your child, take turns naming as many words that begin with n as you can.

Name _____

▶ Say the name of each picture. If the name **begins** with the sound of the letter in the box, print it on the first line. If it **ends** with that sound, print it on the second line.

1. n

2. l

3. d

4. n

5. d

6. l

7. n

8. d

9. n

10. l

11. d

12. l

Say the names of the pictures in the boxes. Look for these pictures in the big picture. Circle each one. Write the letter of each beginning sound.

1.

d

2.

3.

4.

5.

6.

Initial consonants l, d, n

HOME

Make up riddles for your child to solve using picture names, such as *I have four legs and I bark.* (dog)

Name _____

We watch from the window
As winter winds blow.
We watch from the window,
And wish it would snow.

▶ Window **begins with the sound of w.** Circle **each picture whose name begins with the sound of w.**

1.

2.

3.

4.

5.

6.

7.

8.

9.

Say the name of each picture. If it begins with the sound of **w**, print **w** on the line. Then trace the whole word.

1. _____ agon

2. _____ eel

3. _____ ing

4. _____ atch

5. _____ ave

6. _____ og

7. _____ ey

8. _____ allet

9. _____ eb

HOME

Ask your child to choose two pictures whose names begin with the sound of *w* and use the words in a sentence.

Name_____

Carla has a cape.
She's carrying a cane.
Cory has her dad's coat
To play a dress-up game.

> Cape **begins with the sound of c.**
> Circle **each picture whose name**
> **begins with the sound of c.**

1.

2.

3.

4.

5.

6.

7.

8.

9.

Say the name of each picture. **If** it begins with the **sound** of **c**, print **c** on the line. Then trace the whole word.

1. _____ an

2. _____ ap

3. _____ atch

4. _____ ane

5. _____ og

6. _____ ake

7. _____ ow

8. _____ ar

9. _____ up

10. _____ age

11. _____ um

12. _____ omb

 HOME Ask your child to pick three words from the page that begin with c, then draw a picture showing them.

Name_____

The roses are red.
The ribbon is, too.
I ran over to bring
These red roses to you.

Roses **begins with the sound of r.**
Circle **each picture whose name**
begins with the sound of r.

1.

2.

3.

4.

5.

6.

7.

8.

9.

The sound of r: Phonemic awareness   **45**

Say the name of each picture. If it begins with the sound of **r**, print **r** on the line. Then trace the whole word.

1. ing

2. ake

3. ip

4. at

5. at

6. en

7. adio

8. ips

9. ain

10. ug

11. ake

12. eb

The sound of r: Sound to symbol

HOME

Point to the ring picture and ask your child, *What rhymes with king?* Repeat with rhymes for *rip*, *rat*, and *rug*.

Name _____

Penny passed the peach pie,
Peach pie, peach pie.
Penny passed the peach pie,
Till not a piece was left.

▶ **Peach begins with the sound of p.** Circle **each**
picture whose name begins with the sound of p.

1.

2.

3.

4.

5.

6.

7.

8.

9.

Say the name of each picture. If it begins with the sound of **p**, print **p** on the line. Then trace the whole word.

1.

___ot

2.

___up

3.

___ig

4.

___ine

5.

___oap

6.

___en

7.

___urse

8.

___in

9.

___eas

10.

___ap

11.

___at

12.

___ie

 HOME With your child, make up a silly sentence using three words from the page that begin with *p*.

Name_____

Quinn's toy duck said,
"Quack, quack, quack!"
"Quiet!" said Quincy.
But the duck quacked back!

▶ **Quack begins with the sound of qu. Say the name of each picture. If it begins with the sound of qu, print qu on the line.**

1.

2.

3.

4.

5.

6.

7.

8.

The sound of qu: Sound to symbol   **49**

Viv has a valentine.
Val has one, too.
Vic makes a valentine
To give to you.

▶ **Valentine begins with the sound of v.** Say the name of each picture. If it begins with the sound of v, print **Vv** on the line.

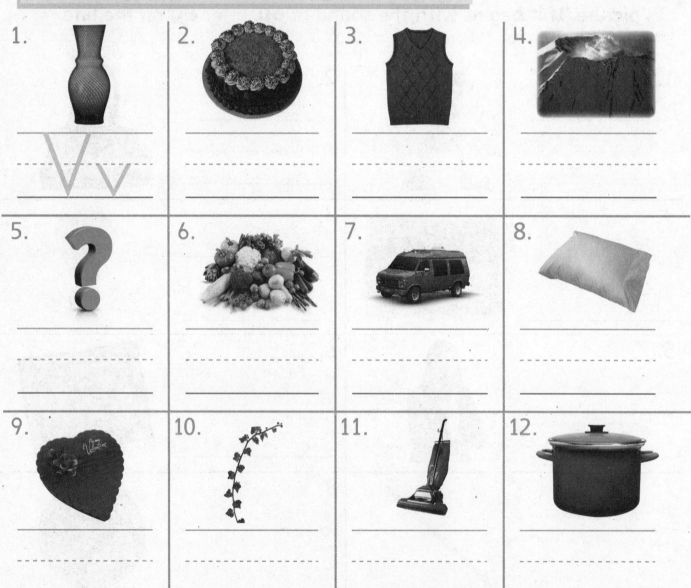

1. ___ Vv ___

2. _____

3. _____

4. _____

5. _____

6. _____

7. _____

8. _____

9. _____

10. _____

11. _____

12. _____

With your child, make up a story using some of the words from the page that begin with v.

Name_____

> Say the name of each picture. Print the letter for its beginning sound on the first line. Then print the letter for its ending sound on the second line.

1.

r n

2.

3.

4.

5.

6.

7.

8.

9.

10.

11.

12.

Say each picture name. **Write** the word that names each picture. What is the secret message?

1. h _ o _ _

2. _ h a _ _

3. _ _ a n _

4. _ e b _ _

5. _ f i _ e

6. _ u e e n _

7. _ n e _

 Ask your child what the secret message is.

Name_____

Will Foxie Fox and Oxie Ox
Fit inside our big toy box?
Mix things up and push and pull.
Fox and Ox make the toy box full!

▶ **Box** ends with the sound of **x.** Say the name
of each picture. If it ends with the sound of
x, print **Xx** on the line.

1. Xx	2.	3.
4.	5. **6**	6.
7.	8. ⭐	9.

Yesterday I went shopping
With my Grandma Lin.
I got a yellow yo-yo.
You can watch it spin.

Yo-yo **begins with the sound of y.** Say **the name of each picture. If it begins with the sound of y, print Yy on the line.**

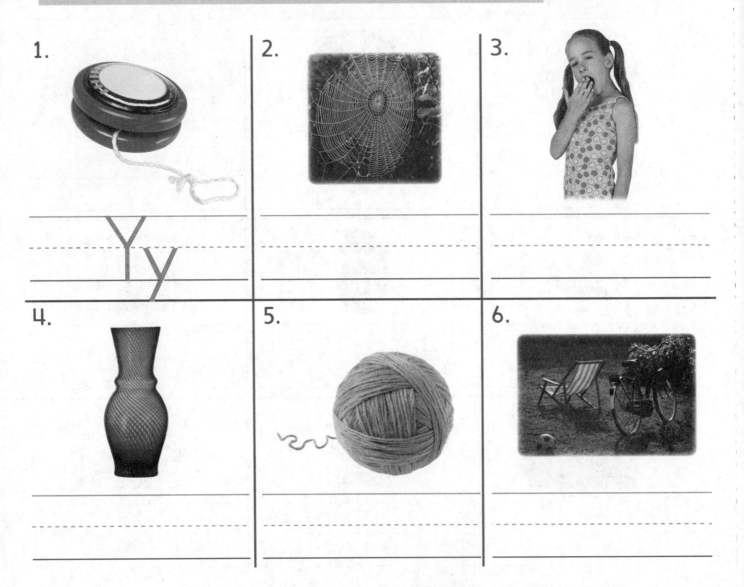

1.

2.

3.

4.

5.

6.

Say, "In my yard, I have a _____." Ask your child to finish the sentence with words that begin with y.

Name_____

Zelda and Zena
Went to the zoo.
There they saw zebras
And lions, too.

▶ **Zoo** begins with the sound of **z**. Say the name of each picture. If it begins with the sound of **z**, print **Zz** on the line.

1.

Zz

2.

3.

4.

5.

6.

Say the name of each picture. If the name begins with the sound of the letter in the box, print it on the first line. If it ends with that sound, print it on the second line.

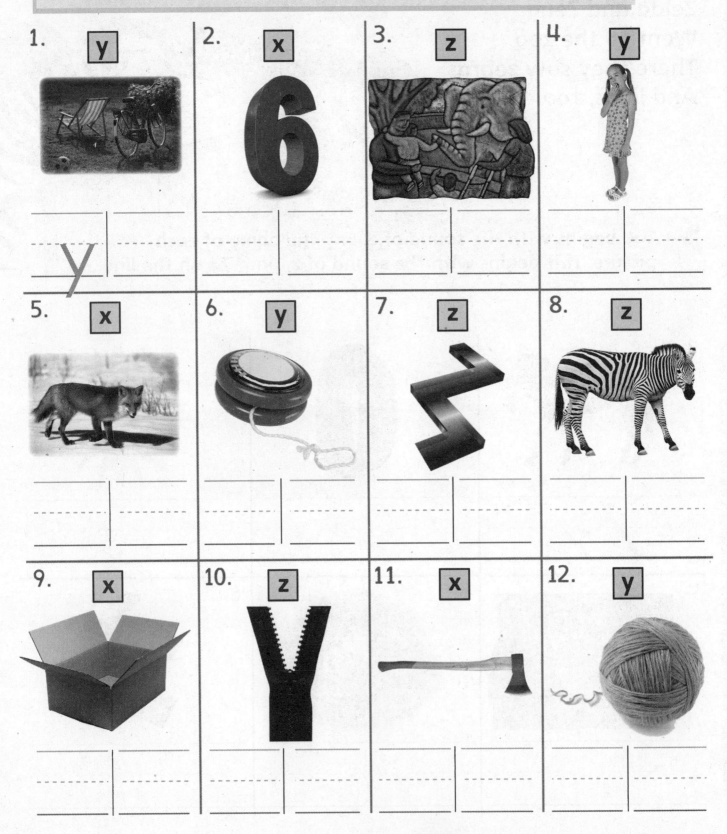

1. y

5. x

9. x

2. x

6. y

10. z

3. z

7. z

11. x

4. y

8. z

12. y

 HOME

Help your child to think of more words that begin or end with x, y, or z, such as x-ray, play, and zip.

Name_____

> Say the name of each picture. Print the letter for its middle sound on the line.

1. _____

2. _____

3. _____

4. _____

5. _____

6. _____

7. _____

8. _____

9. _____

10. _____

11. _____

12. _____

Say the name of each picture. Print the letter for its middle sound on the line. Trace the whole word.

1.

ba __ y

2.

po __ y

3.

ra __ io

4.

wa __ on

5.

ru __ er

6.

le __ on

7.

se __ en

8.

ro __ ot

9.

ti __ er

 HOME Say each middle sound and ask your child to tell you which picture name or names have that sound.

Name _____

Say the name of each picture. Print the letter for its beginning sound. Then print the letter for its ending sound. The words in the box may help you.

bed	cat	fox	ham	jar	beak
pig	queen	tub	van	web	yard

1.

_____ a _____

2.

_____ i _____

3.

_____ o _____

4.

_____ u _____

5.

_____ e _____

6.

_____ a _____

7.

_____ a _____

8.

_____ e _____

9.

_____ a _____

10.

_____ ea _____

11.

_____ ar _____

12.

_____ uee _____

Review consonants: Spelling **59**

Draw a picture of yourself with your friends. **Write** a sentence about the picture.

Review consonants: Writing

Name _____

Camping Fun

It is fun to camp in a tent.

1

---FOLD---

A dog can camp in a tent, too!

4

A tent can go in the woods
or in a yard.

2

A tent can be big or little.

3

FOLD

Name _____

> Say the name of each picture. Print the letter for the missing sound to finish each word. Trace the whole word.

1.   arn

2.   bu

3.   ase

4.   ha

5.   ire

6.   eart

7.   ug

8.   ebra

9.   pe

10.   ueen

11.   agon

12.   tu

> Say the name of each picture. Fill in the bubble next to the letter or letters that stand for the beginning sound.

1.
- ○ y
- ○ d
- ○ m

2.
- ○ k
- ○ r
- ○ w

3.
- ○ l
- ○ p
- ○ t

4.
- ○ c
- ○ n
- ○ z

5.
- ○ f
- ○ t
- ○ qu

6.
- ○ v
- ○ w
- ○ k

> Say the name of each picture. Fill in the bubble next to the letter that stands for the ending sound.

7.
- ○ k
- ○ z
- ○ x

8.
- ○ g
- ○ c
- ○ z

9.
- ○ n
- ○ p
- ○ r

10.
- ○ f
- ○ n
- ○ q

11.
- ○ d
- ○ t
- ○ j

12.
- ○ k
- ○ l
- ○ w

Read Aloud

Frogs Call

Little frogs call.
They sing a song.
Soon the rain will fall.
Tree frogs like wet places.
They hop and jump.
Some tree frogs are green.
Some are red.
Others are blue or yellow.
You can not touch some
tree frogs.
The wet skin can make you sick!

What can tree frogs do?

Dear Family,

In this unit about "Amazing Animals," your child will learn about the vowels **a, e, i, o,** and **u** and the sounds they make. Many animal names contain short vowels such as cat, hen, pig, fox, and duck. As your child becomes familiar with short vowel sounds, you might try these activities together.

▶ Make a collage of animals whose names have the same short vowel sound. With your child, draw pictures or cut pictures from magazines and glue them on paper, one sheet for each vowel.

▶ Your child might enjoy reading these books with you. Look for them in your local library.

Pet of a Pet by Marsha Hayles
How Chipmunk Got His Stripes by Joseph Bruchac

Sincerely,

_____

Estimada familia:

En esta unidad, que trata de "Animales asombrosos," su hijo/a aprenderá las vocales **a, e, i, o, u** y los sonidos que éstas hacen. Los nombres de muchos animales contienen vocales con sonidos breves, como por ejemplo, cat (gato), hen (gallina), pig (cerdo), fox (zorro), y duck (pato). A medida que su hijo/a se vaya familiarizando con las vocales de sonidos breves, podrían hacer las siguientes actividades juntos.

▶ Hagan un collage de fotos o dibujos de animales cuyos nombres contienen vocales con sonidos breves. Junto con su hijo/a dibujen o recorten fotos de revistas y péguenlos en hojas de papel—una hoja por vocal.

▶ Quizás a su hijo/a le gustaría leer con ustedes los siguientes libros que podrían buscar en su biblioteca local.

Pet of a Pet de Marsha Hayles
How Chipmunk Got His Stripes de Joseph Bruchac

Sinceramente,

_____

Name _____

An ant can dance.
An ant can sing.
An ant can do most anything.

Can you dance?
Can you sing?
Can you do most anything?

▶ **Ant has the short sound of a. Circle each picture whose name has the short sound of a.**

1.

2.

3.

4.

5.

6.

7.

8.

9.

10.

11.

12.

Say the names of the pictures in each row.
Color the pictures whose names rhyme.

1.

2.

3.

4.

5.

68   **Short vowel a: Phonograms/rhyme**

 HOME

Help your child use rhyming words from
the page to make up silly sentences
such as *The rat chased the cat.*

Name _____

> Say **the name of each picture.** Circle **its name.**

1.	2.	3.
bat　bad　bag	ant　wax　ax	nap　can　cat

4.	5.	6.
cab　cap　nap	man　bag　band	tag　rag　tap

7.	8.	9.
fat　fan　tan	had　hand　land	tap　lap　lamp

10.	11.	12.
van　had　ran	bad　cab　dad	pat　pan　ran

Read **the words in the blue box.** Print **a word in the puzzle to name each picture.**

Across →

2.

5.

6.

Down ↓

1.

3.

4.

bag   cat   hand   hat   map   pan

Use **some of the words from the box to write a sentence.**

HOME Make up riddles using some of the words from the box. Ask your child to guess each word.

Name _____

> **Blend** the letter sounds together as you say each word. Then **color** the picture it names.

1.

v
a
n

2.

c
a
p

3.

h
a
m

4.

b
a
t

5.

c
a
n

Blend the letter sounds together as you say each word. Print the word on the line. Draw a line to the picture whose name rhymes.

1. m
ap   map

2. r
at

3. h
am

4. t
ag

5. r
an

6. s
ad

Short vowel a: Blending phonograms

HOME Invite your child to say a picture name and think of as many rhyming words as possible.

Name_____

 Say the name of each picture. Print the letter for its beginning sound. Then print the letter for its ending sound.

1.

c a t

2.

a

3.

a

4.

a

5.

a

6.

a

7.

a

8.

a

9.

a

10.

a

11.

a

12.

a

13.

a

14.

a

15.

a

16.

a

Short vowel a: Spelling   **73**

▶ Look at the picture. Circle the word that will finish the sentence. Print it on the line.

1. Max is my _____.

cat
sat
can

2. He licks my _____.

land
hand
ham

3. Max sits on my _____.

pad
rap
lap

4. He likes my _____.

sad
dad
bad

5. He plays with a _____.

bat
rag
bag

6. Max takes a _____.

nap
cap
cab

 Why does the girl like Max?

 Help your child think of sentences using words from the page to continue the story.

Name _____

 Say the name of each picture. Print the name on the line. In the last box, draw a picture of a short a word. Print the word.

1.

fan

2.

3.

4.

5.

6.

7.

8.

9.

10.

11.

12.

Read **the sentences.** Circle **the word that will finish each sentence.** Print **it on the line.**

_____	can
- - - - - - - - - - - - - - - -	van
1. Jan got in the _____.	cat

_____	cap
- - - - - - - - - - - - - - - -	lamp
2. It was time to go to _____.	camp

_____	tap
- - - - - - - - - - - - - - - -	nap
3. In the van, Jan had a _____.	sat

_____	tag
- - - - - - - - - - - - - - - -	rag
4. At camp, Jan made a name _____.	tan

_____	wag
- - - - - - - - - - - - - - - -	bad
5. Jan made a mask with a _____.	bag

_____	band
- - - - - - - - - - - - - - - -	can
6. Jan played in the _____.	hand

 Do you think Jan had fun at camp? Why?

 Ask your child questions that can be answered with words on the page, such as *Jan was sleepy so she took a _____.* (nap)

Name_____

> **Read the story. Use short a words to finish the sentences.**

Go, Ant!

The cat takes a nap.
The ant runs fast.
The ant is on the cat.
The cat is up!

The cat taps the ant.
Go, ant, go!
The cat can not get the ant.

_____

1. The _____ runs fast.

_____

2. The ant is on the _____.

_____

3. The cat _____ the ant.

 **Why does the cat want
to catch the ant?**

Review short vowel a: Reading, critical thinking   **77**

Use one of the letters to make a word with **an** or **ap**. Write each real word on the lines.

r y c m p

an

1. _____

2. _____

3. _____

4. _____

c l b n t

ap

5. _____

6. _____

7. _____

8. _____

▶ Write a sentence using one of the words you made.

_____

_____

_____

HOME Invite your child to think of more words that end with *an* or *ap* such as *fan, tan, gap, map, rap, zap.*

Name

BATS

Photographs by
Dr. Merlin Tuttle

Written by
Jennifer Jacobson

A bat has fur.

1

FOLD

A bat can go fast.

4

This bat has a red snack.

2

A bat can go far.

3

Name_____

▶

I	the
My	with
here	said

_____

1. Pal got _____ ball.

_____

2. "Run," _____ Dan to Pal.

_____

3. Pal ran _____ the ball.

_____

4. "Now run _____, Pal," said Dan.

_____

5. "_____ dog runs fast," Dan said.

_____

6. "_____ like to play with my dog."

▶ **Unscramble the letters to write a word from the box. The word shapes will help you print the words.**

1. asdi

2. eth

3. hree

4. hwit

5. ym

here   my
said   with
        the

CHECKING

▶ **Put a ✔ next to each word you can read.**

☐ with   ☐ said   ☐ my   ☐ here   ☐ the   ☐ I

HOME Using any two words on the page, help your child make up a sentence, then draw a picture to go with it.

Name _____

A big pink pig
Ate a big fig,
Put on a big wig,
And did a jig.

▶ **Pig has the short sound of i. Circle each picture whose name has the short sound of i.**

1.

2.

3.

4.

5.

6.

7.

8.

9.

10.

11.

12.

Say the names of the pictures in each row.
Color the pictures whose names rhyme.

1.

2.

3.

4.

5.

84   Short vowel i: Phonograms/rhyme

 HOME

With your child, make up silly sentences using the rhyming words from each row.

Name _____

> Say the name of each picture. Circle its name.

1.

pin   wig   pig

2.

six   ax   mix

3.

hid   lid   did

4.

bib   bit   bad

5.

fin   pin   pan

6.

fill   hill   bill

7.

mix   mat   mitt

8.

sing   sank   sink

9.

will   milk   mitt

10.

win   fin   fan

11.

fist   fish   fast

12.

win   wing   ring

Farmer Jill's pigs have short **i** words on them. Help Farmer Jill catch her pigs. **Circle** the short **i** words.

Use some of the short **i** words on the pigs to write a sentence.

Short vowel i: Sound to symbol

HOME With your child, take turns making up poems and rhymes for each short *i* word.

Name _____

> Blend the letter sounds together as you say each word. Then, color the picture it names.

1.

w
i
g

2.

m
a
p

3.

p
i
n

4.

b
i
b

5.

m
a
n

Short vowels a, i: Blending phonemes **87**

Blend the letter sounds together as you say each word.
Print the word on the line. **Draw** a line to the picture it names.

1.

p
ig

_____

_ _ _ _ _ _ _ _ _ _ _ _ _

_____

2.

p
an

_____

_ _ _ _ _ _ _ _ _ _ _ _ _

_____

3.

s
ix

_____

_ _ _ _ _ _ _ _ _ _ _ _ _

_____

4.

c
ap

_____

_ _ _ _ _ _ _ _ _ _ _ _ _

_____

5.

r
at

_____

_ _ _ _ _ _ _ _ _ _ _ _ _

_____

6.

r
ip

_____

_ _ _ _ _ _ _ _ _ _ _ _ _

_____

88   Short vowels a, i: Blending phonograms

Ask your child to think of a
rhyming word for three of the
picture names.

Name _____

Say the name of each picture. Print the letters for its beginning and ending sounds. Trace the whole word.

1.

wig

2.

i

3.

i

4.

i

5.

i

6.

i

7.

i

8.

if

9.

in

10.

il

11.

ip

12.

ri

13.

i

14.

i

15.

is

16.

is

Look **at the picture.** Circle **the word that will finish the sentence.** Print **it on the line.**

1. I got a _____ .

gap
gift
gum

2. Is it a _____ ?

milk
mitt
tip

3. Does it drink _____ ?

milk
mitt
mat

4. Will it fit in a _____ ?

damp
dig
dish

5. Can it swim in the _____ ?

sick
sink
sank

6. It is a _____ !

fist
fast
fish

TALK *About It*
Did you ever get a pet as a gift? Tell about it.

HOME
With your child, pick a word on the page and take turns changing the first letter to make new words, such as *dish—fish*.

Name_____

Say the name of each picture. Print the name on the line. In the last box, draw a picture of a short i word. Print the word.

1.

li d

2.

3.

4.

5.

6.

7.

8.

9.

10.

11.

12.

Read **the sentences.** Circle **the word that will finish each sentence.** Print **it on the line.**

_____ dog

------------------------ dig

1. Jim and Linda were going to _____ . pig

_____ bill

------------------------ hit

2. They went to the top of the _____ . hill

_____ rig

------------------------ big

3. Jim saw a rock that was _____ . bag

_____ tip

------------------------ tap

4. He could just see the _____ . rip

_____ at

------------------------ it

5. Linda's truck moved _____ . if

_____ him

------------------------ her

6. She was glad to help _____ . rim

 What other things can be used to dig?

 With your child, make up sentences with short *i* words such as "With a shovel, I can ___."

Short i: High-frequency words, critical thinking

Name _____

 Read **the story.** Print **short i words to finish the sentences.**

Fish Tale

The big fish has little fins.
The little fish has big fins.
The big fish likes to sing.
The little fish likes to swim.
The big fish sings to his friend.
The little fish waves a fin.

_____

1. The _____ fish has little fins.

_____

2. The big fish likes to _____.

_____

3. The little fish waves a _____.

 Why might the big and little fish be friends?

Review short i: Reading, critical thinking   **93**

Use **one of the letters** to make a word with **ig** or **ing**. Write **each real word on a line.**

b c p f d   r s n k w

_____
ig

1. _____

2. _____

3. _____

4. _____

_____
ing

5. _____

6. _____

7. _____

8. _____

Write **a sentence using one of the words you made.**

_____

_____

_____

HOME Ask your child to guess these words as you say them aloud, stretching out the sounds: j-ig, r-ig, w-ig, th-ing, and br-ing.

Name _____

Fast Pig

This pig can run.

1

--------FOLD--------

The race ends.
The pig in red wins.

4

The race has started.
The pig in red is fast.

2

The pigs zip around the ring.
These pigs can not catch the pig in red.

3

Name_____

▶ Read **the words in the box.** Write a word to finish each sentence.

you	for
like	down
are	do

1. Min and Tim _____ playing in the sand.

2. Min says, "What did I _____ with my ring?"

3. "I will help look _____ it," Tim says.

4. Min and Tim look _____ in the sand.

5. "This looks _____ the ring," says Tim.

6. "Tim, _____ are my friend," says Min.

Write **the letter to finish each word.**
Then **print the words on the lines.**

down   are   for   do   like   you

1. d
2. d
   w
   n

3. a
   r
4. l i k

5. y
6. f r
   u

1. _____

2. _____

3. _____

4. _____

5. _____

6. _____

Put a ✔ next to each word you can read.

☐ like   ☐ down   ☐ you   ☐ are   ☐ for   ☐ do

HOME   Help your child make up sentences using the words on this page.

Name_____

Rub-a-dub-dub.
The cub is in the tub.
Rub-a-dub-dub.
The cub likes to scrub.

▶ Cub **has the short sound of u.**
Circle each picture whose name
has the short sound of u.

1.	2.	3.	4.
5.	6.	7.	8.
9.	10.	11.	12.

Say the names of the pictures in each row.
Color the pictures whose names rhyme.

1.

2.

3.

4.

5.

 Help your child think of more words that rhyme with the ones on this page.

Name _____

Say **the name of each picture.** Circle **its name.**

1.

suds   sand   (sun)

2.

gum   mug   gust

3.

cut   cap   cup

4.

bun   bus   sun

5.

bag   bug   big

6.

but   tab   tub

7.

jug   jack   gum

8.

huts   mugs   nuts

9.

tuck   duck   luck

10.

mug   rug   rag

11.

cub   cup   club

12.

drum   dip   mad

Short vowel u: Sound to symbol   **101**

Help the cub get home. Draw a line **from** the cub to the first word with the short **u** sound. Draw **a line to each short u word.**

fun

dog

jug

bug

cat

jam

nut

fox

bed

tub

rug

Use some of the short u words from the puzzle to **write a sentence.**

With your child, take turns naming short *u* words.

Name _____

▶ **Blend** the letter sounds together as you say each word. Then, **color** the picture it names.

1. b
   u
   g

2. c
   a
   n

3. p
   i
   n

4. t
   u
   b

5. r
   a
   t

6. w
   i
   g

Blend **the letter sounds together as you say each word.** Print **the word on the line.** Draw **a line to the picture it names.**

1.
b
at
_____
- - - - - - - - - - -
_____
●

2.
s
ix
_____
- - - - - - - - - - -
_____
●

3.
r
ug
_____
- - - - - - - - - - -
_____
●

4.
p
ig
_____
- - - - - - - - - - -
_____
●

5.
p
an
_____
- - - - - - - - - - -
_____
●

6.
c
ub
_____
- - - - - - - - - - -
_____
●

104 **Short vowels a, i, u: Blending phonograms**

HOME Help your child make up silly rhymes for these picture names, such as *a cub in a tub*.

Name_____

► Say the name of each picture. Print the letter for its beginning and ending sounds. In the last box, draw a picture of a short u word.

1.

cup

2.

u

3.

u

4.

u

5.

u

6.

u

7.

u

8.

u

9.

u

10.

u

11.

u

12.

u

13.

u

14.

u

15.

u

16.

u

Look **at the picture.** Circle **the word that will finish** the sentence. Print **it on the line.**

1. Gus sits on the _____ .

rub
rug
jug

2. He plays with his _____ .

pup
up
cup

3. Soon Gus sees the _____ .

bud
bug
bus

4. He jumps _____ .

hug
up
cup

5. Gus has to _____ .

rub
fun
run

6. The bus is stuck in the _____ !

mud
mug
hum

 What do you think will happen next?

 Ask your child to raise a hand for the short *u* words as you say, *But the bus was just stuck in the mud for an hour.*

Name _____

> Say the name of each picture. Print the picture name on the line. In the last box, draw a picture of a short **u** word. Print the word.

1.

tub

2.

_____

3.

_____

4.

_____

5.

_____

6.

_____

7.

_____

8.

_____

9.

_____

10.

_____

11.

_____

12.

_____

Read the sentences. Circle the word that will finish each sentence. Print it on the line.

1. Our farm is _____.

fan
fin
fun

2. I look under trees for _____.

nuts
rugs
suns

3. Bugs buzz and _____.

hut
hand
hum

4. The pigs dig in the _____.

must
mud
mug

5. My dog jumps and _____.

runs
rings
cuts

6. He likes the warm _____.

gum
sun
hum

 What are some things you might do at a farm?

 Help your child to make up a sentence using the words *fun* and *sun*, then draw a picture to go with it.

Name _____

Phonics & Reading

▶ Read **the story. Use short u words to finish the sentences.**

A Fuss in a Bus

The bug jumps in the bus.
The pup hums in the bus.
The cub runs in the bus.
"Sit down!" says the driver.
"Do not make such a fuss!"
The bug sits.
The cub sits.
The pup does not hum.
No more fuss in the bus!
Now it can go.

_____
- - - - - - - - - - - - -

1. The _____ jumps in the bus.

_____
- - - - - - - - - - - - -

2. The pup hums in the _____.

_____
- - - - - - - - - - - - -

3. The _____ runs in the bus.

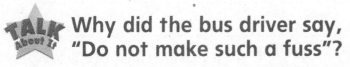

Why did the bus driver say, "Do not make such a fuss"?

Use one of the letters to make a word with un or ug. Write each real word on a line.

brfsl mbkjt

un

1. _____

2. _____

3. _____

4. _____

ug

5. _____

6. _____

7. _____

8. _____

▶ **Write a sentence using one of the words you made.**

_____

_____

_____

Help your child think of other *un* and *ug* words.

Review short vowel u: Phonograms

Name _____

Lunch in a Jug

Make a jug bird feeder.

1

Put nuts and seeds in the jug.
Watch the fun.

4

2

Scrub a jug.
Cut a hole in the jug.

3

Put a string on the jug.
Hang the jug up.

Name_____

My dog has lots of spots.
My dog's spots look like dots.
My dog's spots are on his hair.
My dog's spots are everywhere!

▶ **Spot** has the short sound of **o**. Circle each picture whose name has the short sound of **o**.

1.

2.

3.

4.

5.

6.

7.

8.

9.

10.

11.

12.

Say the names of the pictures in each row.
Color the pictures whose names rhyme.

1.

2.

3.

4.

5.

Short vowel o: Phonograms/rhyme

 HOME With your child, make up action rhymes using short o words from the page, such as *hop with a mop.*

Name_____

 Say the name of each picture. Circle its name.

1.

top   pot   pack

2.

box   fox   fog

3.

log   dog   lot

4.

nap   map   mop

5.

tap   tip   top

6.

hat   hot   hit

7.

dog   dig   dug

8.

bat   box   bug

9.

fill   duck   doll

10.

ox   sock   ax

11.

rip   rack   rock

12.

pop   pup   pat

**Color each short o word red.
What do you see?**

Use some of the short o words in the puzzle to write a sentence.

_____

_ _ _ _ _ _ _ _ _ _ _ _ _ _ _ _ _ _ _

_____

_____

_ _ _ _ _ _ _ _ _ _ _ _ _ _ _ _ _ _ _

_____

Help your child make up a story
using some of the short o words
on the page.

Name_____

 Blend the letter sounds together as you say each word. Color the picture it names.

1. l
   o
   g

2. b
   a
   t

3. c
   u
   b

4. f
   o
   x

5. p
   i
   n

6. r
   u
   g

Blend the letter sounds together as you say each word. **Print** the word on the line. **Draw** a line to the picture it names.

1. b
   ox
   _____

2. s
   ix
   _____

3. c
   up
   _____

4. m
   an
   _____

5. d
   og
   _____

6. b
   us
   _____

Short vowels a, i, u, o: Blending phonograms

Name the beginning letter of a word. Ask your child to say a word that starts with that letter.

▶ Say the name of each picture. Print the letters for its beginning and ending sounds. Trace the word. In the last box, draw a picture of a short **o** word. Print the word.

1.
_____
mop

2.
_____
o

3.
_____
o

4.
_____
o

5.
_____
o

6.
_____
o

7.
_____
o

8.
_____
oc

9.
_____
o

10.
_____
o

11.
_____
ro

12.
_____

Look at the picture. **Circle** the word that will finish the sentence. **Print** it on the line.

1. Bob is _____.

hot
got
hop

2. He sits on top of a _____.

rock
rack
lock

3. He takes off his _____.

sacks
socks
locks

4. The grass is _____.

sack
lift
soft

5. He sees a frog in the _____.

pond
pot
pod

6. The frog hops on a _____.

lock
lost
log

 What do you think Bob might do next?

 With your child, think of silly sentences using the short o words, such as *The frog took off its socks.*

120   Short o: High-frequency words, critical thinking

Name_____

Say the name of each picture. Print the picture name on the line. In the last box, draw a picture of a short o word. Print the word.

1.
_____

2.
_____

3.
_____

4.
_____

5.
_____

6.
_____

7.
_____

8.
_____

9.
_____

10.
_____

11.
_____

12.
_____

Circle the word that will finish the sentence. Print it on the line.

1. Jill likes to _____ .

job
jog
jug

2. She puts on shoes and _____ .

sand
soft
socks

3. She jogs with her _____ .

dot
dock
dog

4. She runs to the _____ of the hill.

top
tap
mop

5. It gets very _____ .

hog
hit
hot

6. She _____ to rest.

sips
stops
steps

 What sports do you like? Why?

 Help your child think of sentences using words from this page to continue the story.

Short o: High-frequency words, critical thinking

Name_____

Read **the story.** Print **short o words to** finish the sentences.

F🐾xes

Foxes live in many places.
Some foxes live where it is hot.
Some live where it is cold.
Foxes are like dogs.
They have soft fur.
A baby fox is called a cub or
a pup.

_____

1. _____ live in many places.

2. Some foxes live where it is _____.

3. Foxes are like _____.

 How is a fox like a dog?

Review short o: Reading, critical thinking   **123**

Phonics & Writing

Use **one of the letters to make a word with ot or og.** Write **each real word on a line.**

l d v p n

ot

1. _____

2. _____

3. _____

4. _____

l m d h f

og

5. _____

6. _____

7. _____

8. _____

▶ Write **a sentence using one of the words you made.**

_____

_____

_____

HOME Help your child think of words that end in *on, od, ox,* and *ob.*

Name _____

In the Tub

A dog and a pup had a bath in a tub.

1

FOLD

Then, the dog and the pup got out and ran!

4

Six hot bugs said, "Can we hop in the tub?"
The dog said, "You can."

2

Six big pigs said, "Can we jump in the tub?"
The dog said, "You can."

3

Review short vowels a, i, u, o: Take-home book

Name _____

▶ Read the words in the box. Write a word to finish each sentence.

of	her
Our	have
one	come

1. _____ family has a pet.

2. We _____ a dog.

3. Molly is _____ name.

4. We could not find Molly _____ day.

5. I said, "Molly, _____ here!"

6. Molly jumped out _____ a box!

► Unscramble the letters to write a word from the box. The word shapes will help you print the words.

1. fo

2. erh

3. uro

4. evha

5. neo

6. moce

have   one   of
our   come   her

CHECKING

► Put a ✔ next to each word you can read.

☐ one   ☐ come   ☐ have   ☐ of   ☐ our   ☐ her

HOME

Name _____

"Red Hen, Red Hen,"
Jen said to her hen.
"Red Hen, Red Hen,
Get back to your pen!"

▶ Hen **has the short sound of e. Circle each picture whose name has the short sound of e.**

1.

2.

3.

→

5.

6.

7.

8.

9.

10.

11.

12.

Say the names of the pictures in each row.
Color the pictures whose names rhyme.

1.

2.

3.

4.

5.

130   Short vowel e: Phonograms/rhyme

 Name a picture. Ask your child to think of words that rhyme.

Name_____

Say the name of each picture. Circle its name.

1.	2.	3.
bed fed led	bill sell bell	tan ten tin

4.	5.	6.
met net nut	west well web	jet pet wet

7.	8.	9.
went man men	leg egg beg	ten tent bent

10.	11.	12.
belt bell melt	pin pet pen	nest not just

▶ **Four red hens are missing from their pen.** Draw a **hen in each box.** Follow the directions **below.**

1.

Draw a hen in a bed.

2.

Draw a hen in a tent.

3.

Draw a hen on a sled.

4.

Draw a hen in a nest.

hen   bed   tent   sled   nest

▶ Use **some of the words from the box to** write **a sentence.**

- -

HOME
Make up riddles using some of the words from the box. Ask your child to guess each word.

Name_____

> **Blend** the letter sounds together as you say each word.
> **Fill in** the bubble under the picture it names.

1. r
   ug
     ○
     ○
     ○

2. t
   en
     ○
     ○
     ○

3. s
   ix
     ○
     ○
     ○

4. h
   at
     ○
     ○
     ○

5. t
   op
     ○
     ○
     ○

6. l
   eg
     ○
     ○
     ○

Blend the sounds together as you say each word. **Print** the word on the line. **Draw** a line to the picture it names.

1.

n

et

_____

2.

m

op

_____

3.

s

un

_____

4.

w

ig

_____

5.

c

at

_____

6.

p

en

_____

 Name a vowel. Ask your child to read a word that has that vowel.

Name _____

> **Say** the name of each picture. **Print** the letter for its beginning and ending sounds. In the last box, **draw** a picture of a short e word.

1. net

2. e

3. e

4. e

5. e

6. e

7. e

8. e

9. en

10. le

11. es

12. el

13. es

14. e

15. es

16. e

Look at the picture. Circle the word that will finish the sentence. Print it on the line.

1. Meg sits at her _____.

mask
desk
duck

2. She picks up her _____.

pen
pet
pig

3. Meg draws a _____.

best
nest
net

4. Then she draws a big _____.

leg
egg
beg

5. On the nest sits a _____.

hen
ten
pen

6. Meg hangs it by her _____.

belt
bell
bed

 What kinds of things do you like to draw?

 Point to the picture of the pen and ask your child to name as many words that rhyme with *pen* as possible.

Short e: High-frequency words, critical thinking

Name_____

 Say the name of each picture. **Print** the picture name on the line. In the last box, **draw** a picture of a short e word. **Print** the word.

1.

_ _ _ _ _ _ _ _ _ _ _ _ _

2.

10

_ _ _ _ _ _ _ _ _ _ _ _ _

3.

_ _ _ _ _ _ _ _ _ _ _ _ _

4.

_ _ _ _ _ _ _ _ _ _ _ _ _

5.

_ _ _ _ _ _ _ _ _ _ _ _ _

6.

_ _ _ _ _ _ _ _ _ _ _ _ _

7.

_ _ _ _ _ _ _ _ _ _ _ _ _

8.

_ _ _ _ _ _ _ _ _ _ _ _ _

9.

_ _ _ _ _ _ _ _ _ _ _ _ _

10.

_ _ _ _ _ _ _ _ _ _ _ _ _

11.

_ _ _ _ _ _ _ _ _ _ _ _ _

12.

_ _ _ _ _ _ _ _ _ _ _ _ _

> Circle **the word that will finish the sentence. Print it on the line.**

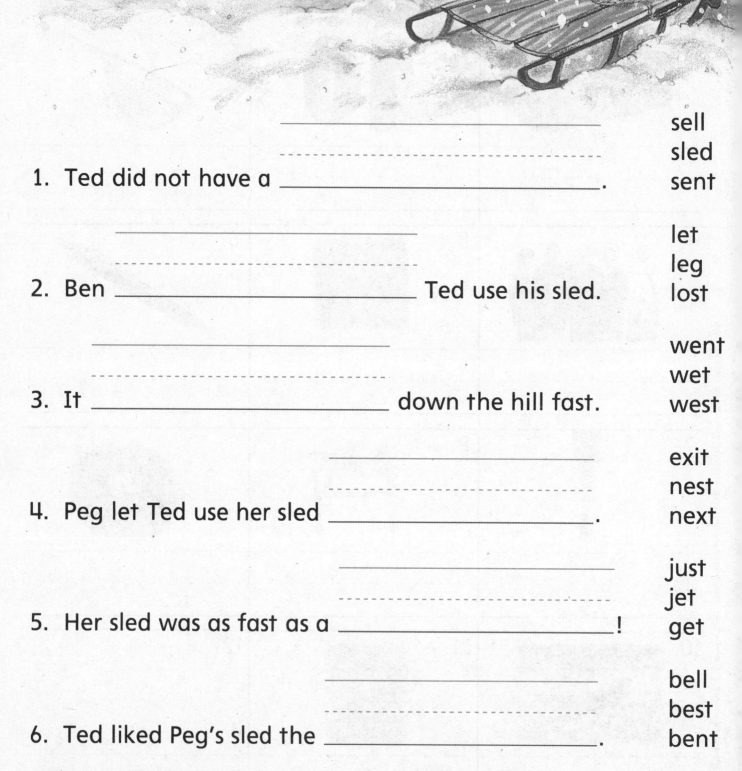

1. Ted did not have a _____ .

sell
sled
sent

2. Ben _____ Ted use his sled.

let
leg
lost

3. It _____ down the hill fast.

went
wet
west

4. Peg let Ted use her sled _____ .

exit
nest
next

5. Her sled was as fast as a _____ !

just
jet
get

6. Ted liked Peg's sled the _____ .

bell
best
bent

 Which sled would you like to use? Why?

 With your child, think of sentences to continue the story using some of the words on the page.

Name _____

 Phonics & Spelling

Say **the name of each picture.** Circle **the vowel you hear in its name.** Print **the word.**

1.

a e i o u

_____

2.

a e i o u

_____

| bag |
| bus |
| lid |
| map |
| pig |
| jet |
| cup |
| sock |

3.

a e i o u

_____

4.

a e i o u

_____

5.

a e i o u

_____

6.

a e i o u

_____

7.

a e i o u

_____

8.

a e i o u

_____

Write a postcard to tell a friend about a trip. Some of the words in the box may help you.

| cat | map | bed | top | bus |
| dog | six | jet | did | sun |

TO:

My Friend
1 Happy Lane
Yourtown,
USA
12345

HOME

Ask your child to use as many of the words in the box as possible in a sentence.

Name _____

Fish Food

What do fish like to eat best?

1

Some fish must hide to get away.
Can you spot a fish here?

4

This fish likes to eat lots of bugs.

2

This fish can fish for small fish.

3

Review short vowels a, i, u, o, e: Take-home book

Name _____

> Say the name of each picture.
> Print the picture name on the line.

1.

bed

2.

3.

4.

5.

6.

7.

8.

9.

10.

11.

12.

▶ **Fill in the bubble beside the sentence that tells about the picture.**

1.
○ One pen is in a box.
○ One pin is in a bag.

2.
○ The gift is here in the bag.
○ The quilt is here on the bed.

3.
○ The man set up the tent.
○ The men are on the bus.

4.
○ Miss Beck runs with the dog.
○ Jeff hugs the cat on the bed.

▶ **Can you read each word? Put a ✔ in the box if you can.**

☐ I	☐ are	☐ of	☐ here	☐ like	☐ one
☐ for	☐ my	☐ her	☐ with	☐ down	☐ come
☐ the	☐ you	☐ our	☐ said	☐ have	☐ do

Play

by Frank Asch

Come play with me said the sun,
Come play with me said the earth,
Come play with me said the sky.
What shall we play said I?

Let's fly a kite said the sun,
Stand on me said the earth,
I'll bring the wind said the sky,
I'll hold the string said I.

TALK About It

What are other fun ways
to play outdoors?

Dear Family,

In this unit called "Let's Play," your child will learn about the sounds of long vowels. Many words related to play contain long vowels, such as skate, feet, bike, boat, and flute. As your child becomes more familiar with vowel sounds, you might try these activities together.

▶ Look through old magazines and catalogs to find and cut out pictures of toys, games, musical instruments, sports events, or sports equipment whose names have long vowel sounds. Ask your child to group the pictures according to the long vowel sounds.

▶ Read the poem on page 145 with your child and help him or her to identify the words with long vowel sounds.

▶ Your child might enjoy reading these books with you. Look for them in your local library.

Ten Minutes Till Bedtime
by Peggy Rathmann

Lentil by Robert McCloskey

Sincerely,

Estimada familia:

En esta unidad, titulada "Juguemos" ("Let's Play"), su hijo/a estudiará los sonidos de las vocales largas en inglés. Muchas palabras relacionadas con actividades de entretenimiento contienen vocales con sonidos largos, como por ejemplo, skate (patín), feet (pies), bike (bicicleta), boat (bote), y flute (flauta). A medida que su hijo/a se vaya familiarizando con los sonidos de las vocales, pueden hacer las siguientes actividades juntos.

▶ Busquen y recorten en revistas y catálogos viejos ilustraciones de juguetes, juegos, instrumentos musicales, eventos o equipos deportivos cuyos nombres contengan vocales con sonidos largos. Pidan a su hijo/a que agrupe las ilustraciones de acuerdo a los sonidos largos de las vocales.

▶ Lean el poema en la página 145 con su hijo/a y ayúdenle a identificar las palabras que contengan vocales con sonidos largos.

▶ Ustedes y su hijo/a disfrutarán leyendo estos libros juntos. Búsquenlos en su biblioteca local.

Ten Minutes Till Bedtime
de Peggy Rathmann

Lentil de Robert McCloskey

Sinceramente,

Unit 3 • Introduction

Name_____

James wants to bake
a big birthday cake.
He plans to make
the cake for Jake.

▶ Bake **has the long sound of a.** Circle **each picture whose name has the long sound of a.**

1.

2.

TOMATOES

3.

4.

5.

6.

7.

8.

9.

10.

11.

12.

Say the names of the pictures in each row.
Color the pictures whose names rhyme.

1.

2.

3.

4.

5.

Long vowel a: Phonograms/rhyme

With your child, make up short rhymes using the rhyming words in each row.

Name_____

Say **the name of each picture.** Circle **its name.**

1.

tape   tail   late

2.

late   lake   rake

3.

nail   rail   name

4.

case   cap   cape

5.

gave   game   name

6.

pill   pail   sail

7.

gate   game   date

8.

pain   ran   rain

9.

van   save   vase

10.

may   hay   way

11.

pail   rain   Gail

12.

play   pay   hay

▶ Help **Jay** get to the game. Read **each word.**
Draw **a line to join the long a words.**

pig   cup

bat   vase

mail   lake

rake

cake   tray

rain

gate   play

▶ Use **some of the long a words to write a sentence.**

_____

_____

_____

With your child, make up a story using
some of the words along the path
that leads to the soccer game.

Name_____

> **Say** the name of each picture. If the vowel sound is **short**, color the box with the word **short**. If the vowel sound is long, color the box with the word **long**.

1.

| short | long |

2.

| short | long |

3.

| short | long |

4.

| short | long |

5.

| short | long |

6.

| short | long |

7.

| short | long |

8.

| short | long |

9.

| short | long |

10.

| short | long |

11.

| short | long |

12.

| short | long |

Help Dave, Gail, and Ray find the long a words.
Circle each one you find.

1.

at	ate	rake	rack	page
made	safe	tap	tape	mad

Dave

2.

rain	ram	wait	cat	pail
sat	sail	main	man	pal

Gail

3.

May	man	pay	pat	play
day	hat	say	way	sand

Ray

152   Long vowel a: Sound to symbol

 With your child, think of sentences using words that rhyme with *Dave, Gail,* and *Ra* such as *Ray wants to play today.*

Name _____

> Say the name of each picture. Circle its name.

1.

rat   rate

2.

pain   pan

3.

tap   tape

4.

can   cane

5.

can   cane

6.

hate   hat

7.

cape   cap

8.

cape   cap

9.

ran   rain

10.

bat   bait

11.

hay   hat

12.

take   tack

Long and short vowel a: Sound to symbol   **153**

Color each balloon that has three rhyming long a words.

1. game tame name

2. take tape ape

3. cane lane mane

4. sail same rail

5. cake rake lake

6. gate date late

7. fade made make

8. cave wave cake

9. bake fake fame

10. nail mail pail

11. rain gain pain

12. hay day pay

HOME

Pick a balloon with three rhyming words. Ask your child to name another word that rhymes.

Name _____

 Say the name of each picture. Print the missing vowels on the line. In the last box, draw a picture of a long a word. Print the word.

1. cape

2. c_n r

3. r_n

4. v_s

5. c_k

6. l_k

7. b_g

8. n_l

9. g_m

10. p_l

11. g_t

12.

Look at the picture. Circle the word that will finish each sentence. Print it on the line.

1. _____ and Ray go out to play.

Save
Dave
Sand

2. They go to the _____.

lake
make
late

3. They play a _____.

gate
name
game

4. Ray sits by a _____.

save
came
cave

5. Dave sees a boat with a _____.

save
sail
mail

6. They go in when it _____.

rains
cane
ran

 What are some things you might do at a lake?

Ask your child to use the words circled on this page in sentences.

Name _____

Say the name of each picture. Print the picture name on the line. In the last box, draw a picture of a long a word. Print the word.

1.

_____

2.

_____

3.

_____

4.

_____

5.

_____

6.

_____

7.

_____

8.

_____

9.

_____

10.

_____

11.

_____

12.
_____

Circle **the word that will finish the sentence.**
Print **it on the line.**

lane
late
lake

1. The bus was _____.

wait
wade
wake

2. Mom had to _____.

rate
rake
rain

3. Then, she ran home in the _____.

gain
gate
game

4. Mom came in by the _____.

gave
gain
gate

5. She _____ me a big hug.

made
mail
make

6. I gave her the _____.

 Do you think Mom was glad to be home? Why?

 With your child, continue the story using some of the words printed on this page.

158 Long a: High-frequency words, critical thinking

Name _____

Read **the story.** Use **long a words to finish the sentences.**

Hooray For Ray!

It was the day of the big game.
Ray was at bat.
The ball came at him.
Ray gave the ball a big whack!
Ray raced around the bases.
He came to home plate.
"Safe!"
"Hooray for Ray!"

1. It was the day of the big _____.

2. Ray raced around the _____.

3. He was _____ at home _____.

How do you think Ray felt as he raced around the bases? Why?

Review long vowel a: Reading, critical thinking   **159**

Use **one of the letters to make a word with** **ay** or **ail**. Write **each real word on the lines.**

d s p h v

ay

1. _____

2. _____

3. _____

4. _____

p m s y n

ail

5. _____

6. _____

7. _____

8. _____

▶ Write **a sentence using one of the words you made.**

_____

_____

_____

HOME Help your child think of other long vowel *a* words, such as *race* and *grape*.

Name _____

Make a Face

It is fun to make a clown face.

1

Now you can play!

4

2 You will need some face paint.

3 Start by making shapes.

Name_____

> Read the words in the box. Write a word to finish each sentence.

They	Where
out	two
were	your

_____

1. Kate and Jay _____ at the beach.

2. Dad took them _____ to play in the waves.

3. "I see _____ fish," said Kate.

4. " _____ are the fish?" Jay said.

5. Dad said, "They are by _____ feet."

6. _____ jumped in the waves all day.

Look **at the picture. Then,** print **words from the box to finish the story. The word shapes will help you.**

They	were	two
out	Where	your

1. [_____] did the cat and dog go to play?

2. [_____] went to the beach.

3. Soon the [_____] friends [_____] hot.

4. The dog went to swim [_____] in the waves.

5. "Do not shake [_____] waves on me!" said the cat.

CHECKING UP

▶ Put a ✔ next to each word you can read.

☐ they ☐ were ☐ where ☐ out ☐ two ☐ your

HOME Help your child retell the story, using some of the new words.

Name_____

I ride my bike.
I fly a kite.
I take a hike.
Then, I say good night!

 Ride has the long sound of i. Circle **each picture whose name has the long sound of i.**

1.

2.

3.

4.

5.

6.

7.

8.

9.

10.

11.

12.

Say the names of the pictures in each row.
Color the pictures whose names rhyme.

1.

2.

3.

4.

5.

6.

 HOME

Point to a picture and ask your child to name it. Taking turns, try to say as many rhyming words as you can.

Name _____

▶ **Say the name of each picture. Circle its name.**

1.

mine   nine   vine

2.

dive   dine   dime

3.

pin   pie   pine

4.

ride   hide   ripe

5.

bite   bike   kite

6.

fine   fire   five

7.

tie   ride   tire

8.

bite   tide   bike

9.

like   kite   tile

10.

_____

vine   wine   line

11.

dive   dime   five

12.

hide   ride   hit

Long vowel i: Sound to symbol   **167**

Read the words in the box. **Print** a word in the puzzle to name each picture.

tie	bike	ride	ice
kite	mice	pie	dime

Across ➤

1.

3.

4.

7.

8.

Down ⬇

2.

5.

6.

Use some of the words from the box to write a sentence.

168   Long vowel i: Sound to symbol

HOME

Help your child make up a short poem using some of the long *i* words.

Name_____

> Say the name of each picture. If the vowel sound is short, color the box with the word **short**. If the vowel sound is long, color the box with the word **long**.

1.

short	long

2.

short	long

3.

short	long

4.

short	long

5.

short	long

6.

short	long

7.

short	long

8.

short	long

9.

short	long

10.

short	long

11.

short	long

12.

short	long

Say the name of each picture. Circle its name.

1.

rid   ride

2.

kit   kite

3.

pin   pine

4.

cap   cape

5.

dim   dime

6.

rip   ripe

7.

lid   lied

8.

ran   rain

9.

fin   fine

10.

bit   bite

11.

Tim   time

12.

slid   slide

 HOME

With your child, make up sentences using the short and long vowel words, such as *The shark's fin is fine.*

Name _____

> Say the name of each picture. Print the missing vowels on the line. Trace the whole word.

1.

r _ d

2.

p _ g

3.

d _ m _

4.

f _ r

5.

_ _ n

6.

h _ v _

7.

_ _ d

8.

k _ t _

9.

f _ v _

10.

b _ k _

11.

d _ v _

12.

s _ x

Long and short vowel i: Spelling   **171**

> **Look** at the picture. **Circle** the word that will finish the sentence. **Print** it on the line.

1. **5** Jim has _____ dimes.

   fine
   file
   five

2. He will not get a _____.

   kite
   bite
   bake

3. He will not get a _____.

   lie
   pie
   pile

4. First, Jim waits in _____.

   like
   lied
   line

5. He has fun on the _____.

   rise
   ripe
   ride

6. He rides home on his _____.

   take
   bike
   bite

 Why do you think Jim chose the ride?

 Help your child think of sentences using words from the page to continue the story.

Name _____

> Say the name of each picture. Print the name on the line. In the last box, draw a picture of a long i word. Print the word.

1.

bike

2.

3.

4.

5.

6.

7.

8.

9.

10.

11.

12.

▶ Circle **the word that will finish the sentence.**
Print **it on the line.**

1. Mike likes his _____.

bite
bike
bake

2. It has a nine on the _____.

side
sale
sand

3. It is the same size as _____.

miss
mine
mitt

4. Mike will _____ it in the race.

ride
ripe
rake

5. The race is six _____ long!

miss
mills
miles

6. Last time it ended in a _____.

tie
tide
tip

 **How does it feel when
you win a race?**

 Help your child make up a sentence
that uses any two circled words, then
draw a picture that goes with it.

Name _____

Read **the story.** Use **long i words to finish the sentences.**

Flying a Kite

Children in many places like to fly kites.
In Japan, children fly kites on New Year's day.
The kites can come in many shapes and sizes.
Children tie on a string.
The kites dive and glide.
Hold on to the line!

1. Children in many places like to fly _____.

2. Children _____ on a string.

3. The kites _____ and glide.

 Can you think of more shapes and sizes for kites?

Phonics & Writing

Use **one of the letters** to make a word with **ide** or **ine**. Write **each real word on the lines.**

r s w h y

_____ ide

1. _____

2. _____

3. _____

4. _____

n m b f l

_____ ine

5. _____

6. _____

7. _____

8. _____

Write a sentence using one of the words you made.

_____

_____

_____

Review long vowel i: Phonograms

HOME
Help your child make up a sentence using as many long vowel *i* words as you can.

Name _____

Di Tries

"I can hike a mile," said Ray.

1

Dad hiked a mile, and Di took a ride. That made Ray smile!

4

"I may hike a mile, too," said Di.

2

"You can try," Ray said. "Fine," said Di. "Make way!"

3

Name_____

> Read **the words in the box.** Write a word to finish each sentence.

long	there
Why	little
could	about

_____

1. _____ was Maya smiling?

2. She was thinking _____ her pets.

3. She had two _____ white mice.

4. The mice had _____ tails.

5. Maya _____ hold them in her hands.

6. The mice liked to be _____ .

Look at the picture. Then, print words from the box to finish the story. The word shapes will help you.

| long | Could | little |
| Why | there | about |

1. ☐☐☐ are we going in the car?

2. We are taking a ☐☐☐☐☐☐ trip.

3. It is ☐☐☐☐☐ five miles ☐☐☐☐ .

4. ☐☐☐☐☐ that be the place?

5. Yes, ☐☐☐☐☐ is the pet store!

CHECKING

Put a ✔ next to each word you can read.

☐ long ☐ could ☐ little ☐ why ☐ there ☐ about

HOME Help your child use the boxed words to make up sentences, such as *The little mouse is nice.*

Name_____

Lu used a tube
Of strong white glue
To paste her cube
On top of Sue's.

 Tube **has the long sound of u. Circle each picture whose name has the long sound of u.**

1.

2.

3.

4.

5.

6.

7.

8.

9.

10.

11.

12.

Say the names of the pictures in each row.
Color the pictures whose names rhyme.

1.

2.

3.

4.

5.

Long and short vowel u: Phonograms/rhyme

 HOME

With your child, make up a sentence that rhymes for each row of rhyming pictures, such as *I sang a tune in June.*

Name_____

> Say the name of each picture. Circle its name.

1.

rule   mule   rude

2.

cup   cube   cub

3.

cute   cube   cub

4.

tub   tube   tug

5.

tune   tube   tub

6.

Sue   due   fuss

7.

use   sit   suit

8.

June   tune   nuts

9.

use   sun   suit

10.

tune   tube   tuck

11.

run   bun   rude

12.

fun   suit   fruit

Read **each sentence.** Use **the code to make each pair of words.** Print **them on the lines. Then,** circle **the word that finishes the sentence.**

1 = a	2 = e	3 = i	4 = u	5 = b	6 = c
7 = f	8 = l	9 = m	10 = r	11 = s	12 = t

1. June plays the _____ _____ .

   12 4 5 1   10 4 8 2

2. Luke will feed his _____ _____ .

   7 8 4 12 2   9 4 8 2

3. Sue likes to eat _____ _____ .

   6 4 5 2   7 10 4 3 12

4. Ben got a new _____ _____ .

   11 4 3 12   6 8 4 2

DUKE

5. Duke's house is _____ _____ .

   12 10 4 2   5 8 4 2

HOME

Make up riddles using the long vowel *u* words from the page. Ask your child to guess each word.

Name_____

> Say the name of each picture. If the vowel sound is short, color the box with the word **short**. If the vowel sound is long, color the box with the word **long**.

1.

| short | long |

2.

| short | long |

3.

| short | long |

4.

| short | long |

5.

| short | long |

6.

| short | long |

7.

| short | long |

8.

| short | long |

9.

| short | long |

10.

| short | long |

11.

| short | long |

12.

| short | long |

> **Color** the bubble blue if it has three long **u** words in it.

1. rude
Sue
tune

2. suit
tune
fruit

3. mule
use
cube

4. fire
tire
ride

5. blue
rule
Sue

6. cute
mute
cube

7. pail
sail
tail

8. mile
file
pile

9. rug
tug
mug

> **Use** some of the long vowel **u** words on this page to write a sentence.

_____

- -

_____

_____

- -

_____

HOME

Point to a bubble and say the words inside. With your child, take turns naming other words with the long or short vowel sound.

Name_____

▶ **Say** the name of each picture. **Circle** its name.

1.

tub   tube

2.

tub   tube

3.

pin   pine

4.

dim   dime

5.

cub   cube

6.

cub   cube

7.

ran   rain

8.

cut   cute

9.

rid   ride

10.

hat   hate

11.

cape   cap

12.

kit   kite

Look at the picture. Circle the word that will finish the sentence. Print it on the line.

1. Luke will _____ a box.

us
use
tune

2. The box looks like a

_____ .

cute
cube
cub

3. He got it from _____ .

rule
Sue
due

4. Luke has a

_____ of glue in it.

tune
tub
tube

5. He will put a

_____ in it, too.

ruler
rude
rubs

6. Luke will take it on the

_____ .

suit
bun
bus

 Where do you think Luke is taking the box?

 Help your child to think of a sentence that uses some of the long *u* words on the page.

Long and short vowel u: High-frequency words, critical thinking

Name_____

> Say the name of each picture. Print the missing vowels on the line. Trace the whole word.

1.

c _ b

2.

t _ l

3.

J _ n

4.

f _ v

5.

l _ k

6.

t _ b

7.

k _ t

8.

s _ t

9.

g _ m

10.

c _ p

11.

m _ l

12.

t _ n

Long and short vowels a, i, u: Spelling   **189**

Circle **the word that will finish the sentence.**
Print **it on the line.**

1. Sue has a _____.

must
mule
mile

2. Is a mule a _____ pet?

cute
cube
cut

3. Will she ride it in _____?

jug
tune
June

4. Does the mule like to eat _____?

fun
fruit
rule

5. I do not have a _____.

cute
clue
cuts

6. I want to ask _____.

sun
Sue
suit

 **Where do you think Sue lives?
Why do you think that?**

 Help your child to continue the story using some of the circled words on the page.

Name _____

> Say the name of each picture. Print the name on the line. In the last box, draw a picture of a long u word. Print the word.

1.

cube

2.

_____

3.

_____

4.

_____

5.

_____

6.

_____

7.

_____

8.

toothpaste

_____

9.

_____

10.

_____

11.

_____

12.

_____

▶ Circle the long **a**, long **i**, and long **u** words
in the puzzle. The words in the box will help you.

r	a	i	n
s	u	i	t
r	a	c	a
t	i	e	p
m	u	l	e

rain	ice	tape
suit	tie	mule

▶ Print the word from the box that names each picture.

1. _____

2. _____

3. _____

4. _____

5. _____

6. _____

Ask your child to use three of the words from the box in a sentence.

Name _____

Read **the story.** Use **long u words to finish the sentences.**

The **Blue** Suit

A cute cub saw some fruit.
The fruit was blue.
"This fruit looks good,"
said the cub.
He ate the fruit.
He hummed a tune.
Blue juice got all over him.
"Look!" said the cub's dad.
"You have a new blue suit!"

_____

1. The _____ was blue.

_____

2. Blue _____ got on the cub.

_____ _____

3. The cub had a new _____ _____.

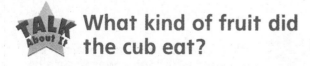

What kind of fruit did the cub eat?

Use **one of the letters to make a word with**
une or ule. Write each real word on the lines.

j d b t

m l r v

une

ule

1. _____

2. _____

3. _____

4. _____

5. _____

▶ **Write a sentence using one of the words you made.**

_____

_____

_____

_____

HOME
Ask your child questions that can be
answered with long *u* words, such as
"What word means song?" (tune)

Name _____

Hand Games

------FOLD------

You can use your hands to make pictures. Shine a light on a wall.

1

Hold up two hands and move them. Make a bird that can fly!

4

Review long vowels a, i, u: Take-home book **195**

2 Make a cute rabbit. Hold up one hand this way.

3 Make a huge white swan. Hold up one hand like this.

Name_____

Turn the jump rope,
High, low, fast, slow!
Put on a show!
Come on, let's go!

 Rope **has the long sound of o.** Circle **each picture whose name has the long sound of o.**

1.

2.

3.

4.

5.

6.

7.

8.

9.

10.

11.

12.

Say the names of the pictures in each circle. Color the parts of the circle that have pictures with long **o** names.

1.

2.

3.

4.

Use **some of the long o words to write a sentence.**

_____

_____

_____

_____

198 Long vowel o: Sound to symbol

Name _____

> **Say** the names of the pictures in each row.
> **Color** the pictures whose names rhyme.

1.

2.

3.

4.

5.

Say **the name of each picture.** Circle **its name.**

1.

coat   cat   coal

2.

ripe   rope   rip

3.

name   rose   nose

4.

sap   soap   sop

5.

boat   bat   toad

6.

robe   rob   bone

7.

rain   cone   cane

8.

doe   hoe   toe

9.

gate   goat   got

10.

row   bow   toe

11.

hose   hope   hot

12.

cone   boat   bone

 HOME

Help your child think of other words that rhyme with the names of the pictures on this page, such as *nose, rose, toes.*

Name _____

> Say the name of each picture. Circle the letters that make the long sound of o.

1.

g o a t

2.

b o w

3.

n o s e

4.

c o n e

5.

r o p e

6.

b o a t

7.

n o t e

8.

r o w

9.

s o a p

10.

h o s e

11.

c o a t

12.

bone

Look at the picture. Then, follow the directions below.

Directions

1. Color the hose green.
2. Color the boat blue.
3. Circle the girl who will row.
4. Draw a toad on the stone.

5. Make an X on the hoe.
6. Color the roses red.
7. Draw a hole for the mole.
8. Draw a rope on the goat.

With your child, make up a story about the picture using the long o words.

Name _____

> Say the name of each picture. If the vowel sound is short, color the box with the word **short**. If the vowel sound is long, color the box with the word **long**.

1. | short | long |

2. | short | long |

3. | short | long |

4. | short | long |

5. | short | long |

6. | short | long |

7. | short | long |

8. | short | long |

9. | short | long |

10. | short | long |

11. | short | long |

12. | short | long |

Say the name of each picture. Circle the words in the boxes that rhyme with the picture name.

1.

bone	cane	loan	moan	can
Joan	tone	run	zone	coat

2.

got	boat	coat	note	vote
rate	cute	tote	gate	moat

3.

snow	doe	tip	top	slow
go	tube	row	foe	tail

4.

rope	slow	blow	rip	snow
low	ride	bow	tow	rock

204 Long vowel o: Sound to symbol

Help your child to make up sentences using the rhyming words, such as *I wore a coat in the boat.*

Name_____

> Say the name of each picture. Circle its name.

1. cat coat	**2.** not note	**3.** mop mope	**4.** kit kite
5. bat boat	**6.** rob robe	**7.** got goat	**8.** cub cube
9. sap soap	**10.** rat rate	**11.** moan man	**12.** cute cut

Look **at the picture.** Circle **the word that will finish the sentence.** Print **it on the line.**

1. A mole hides in a _____.

hose
hole
hope

2. A fish swims in a _____.

box
bone
bowl

3. A goat eats a _____.

bone
cone
cane

4. A cat goes up a _____.

poke
pole
loan

5. A dog begs for a _____.

bone
robe
boat

6. A fox cleans its _____.

cone
coal
coat

 Which animals make good pets? Why?

 Ask your child to use the words circled on this page in sentences.

Long vowel o: High-frequency words, critical thinking

Name _____

> Say the name of each picture. Print the missing vowels on the line. Trace the whole word.

1.

c ___ n

2.

h ___ s ___

3.

r ___ b ___

4.

t ___ p

5.

r ___ p ___

6.

c ___ ___ t

7.

n ___ t ___

8.

n ___ s ___

9.

s ___ ___ p

10.

p ___ t

11.

m ___ p

12.

b ___ ___ t

Circle the word that will finish the sentence. Print it on the line.

road
robe
role

1. The store is up the _____ .

_____

song
soak
soap

2. Joan goes in and smells the _____ .

_____

not
nose
hope

3. It gets on her _____ .

_____

boss
bow
row

4. Joan sees a red _____ .

_____

robe
rob
ripe

5. She sees a blue _____ , too.

_____

hose
hole
home

6. She will pay and take them _____ .

 THINK What kind of store did Joan visit?

 HOME With your child, think of other sentences using these long o words.

Name _____

Say the name of each picture. Print the name on the line. In the last box, draw a picture of a long o word. Print the word.

1.

bone

2.

3.

4.

5.

6.

7.

8.

9.

10.

11.

12.

Say each picture name. Draw a line through the three pictures in a row that have the same long vowel sound.

Review long vowels a, i, u, o: Sound to symbol

 Ask your child to think of more words using the long vowel a, i, u, or o that "won" in each puzzle.

Name_____

Read the story. Use long o words to finish the sentences.

Joe's Show

Joe wanted to put on a show.
"My dog Bo will be in the
show," he said.
"Bo can catch a bone."
Joe's friend Rose came by.
"Can my dog Moe be in your
show?" Rose asked.
"He knows how to roll over,"
she said.
"Yes," said Joe.
Moe and Bo were stars!

1. Joe wanted to put on a _____.

2. Bo can catch a _____.

3. Moe knows how to _____ over.

 What other tricks can
pets do?

Use **one of the letters to make a word with ose or old.** Write **each real word on the lines.**

r h n f p

g s c p h

ose

1. _____

2. _____

3. _____

4. _____

old

5. _____

6. _____

7. _____

8. _____

Write **a sentence using one of the words you made.**

_____

_____

_____

Ask your child to put two thumbs up for a rhyming pair; then, say word pairs such as *rose–hose* or *sold–stop*.

Name _____

Games Around the Globe

Children around the globe like to play games.

1

FOLD

Children in many places like to jump rope. What kind of games do you like to play?

4

Some children play ball games. They must know the rules of the game.

2

Some children like to play clapping games. They can clap and sing a tune.

3

Name_____

> Read the words in the box. Write a word to finish each sentence.

from	which
them	because
Their	want

1. Joe could not go out _____ of the rain.

2. "Do you _____ to call Cody or Flo?"
Mom said.

3. Joe did not know _____ friend to call.

4. Mom said Joe could call both of _____.

5. They played a game _____ Mexico.

6. _____ game was fun!

► Look at the picture. Then, print words from the box to finish the story. The word shapes will help you.

from	their	because
them	Which	want

1. Lin and Lola know Joel ☐☐☐☐ school.

2. They ☐☐☐☐ him to be ☐☐☐☐☐ friend.

3. Joel used to say, "☐☐☐☐☐ twin is which?"

4. Now he can tell ☐☐☐☐ apart.

5. He knows ☐☐☐☐☐☐ Lin has a gold cap.

CHECKING UP

► Put a ✔ next to each word you can read.

☐ them   ☐ want   ☐ because   ☐ which   ☐ from   ☐ their

HOME Help your child to make up a sentence using some of the words in the box.

Name_____

Here in my tree
Is the best place to be.
I can see down,
But the green leaves
Hide me!

▶ Tree **has the long sound of e.** Circle **each picture whose name has the long sound of e.**

1.	2.	3.	4.
5.	6.	7.	8.
9.	10.	11.	12.

Say the names of the pictures in each row.
Color the pictures whose names rhyme.

1.

2.

3.

4.

5.

218   Long vowel e: Phonograms/rhyme

HOME With your child, take turns naming the
first picture in a row and saying a new
word that rhymes, such as *wheel, feel*.

Name _____

▶ **Say the name of each picture. Circle its name.**

1.

beet   feed   feet

2.

leaf   lead   feel

3.

meat   seat   seed

4.

feel   heel   heat

5.

see   tea   bee

6.

real   seat   seal

7.

jeep   Jean   peep

8.

beep   peel   reel

9.

beam   seem   team

10.

bead   jeans   bean

11.

need   seed   seal

12.

beads   bean   beep

Help **Jean and Lee find the seals at the zoo.** Read each word. Draw a line to join the long e words.

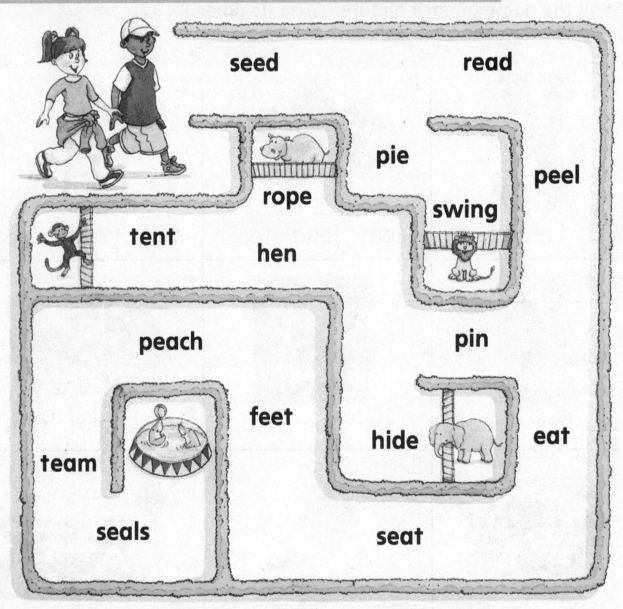

seed   read

pie   peel

rope   swing

tent   hen

peach   pin

feet

team   hide   eat

seals   seat

Use **some of the long e words to write a sentence.**

 Help your child to use some of the words along the path to make up a short story.

Name_____

> Say the name of each picture. If the vowel sound is short, color the box with the word **short**. If the vowel sound is long, color the box with the word **long**.

1.

| short | long |

2.

| short | long |

3.

| short | long |

4.

| short | long |

5.

| short | long |

6.

| short | long |

7.

| short | long |

8.

| short | long |

9.

| short | long |

10.

| short | long |

11.

| short | long |

12.

| short | long |

> Say **the name of each picture.** Circle **the words in the boxes that rhyme with the picture name.**

1.

me	team	see	met	bean
he	we	fee	tea	seed

2.

feel	seal	sell	deep	deal
men	meal	real	leaf	help

3.

feet	beat	bet	heat	set
seat	net	neat	peat	wet

4.

please	pegs	feet	meats	fleas
seals	teas	begs	deep	team

Ask your child to clap for a rhyming pair; then, say word pairs from the page, such as *me, see* and *tea, met*.

Name_____

> Say the name of each picture. Circle its name.

1.

bed   bead

2.

met   meat

3.

neat   net

4.

kite   kit

5.

ten   teen

6.
set   seat

7.

mean   men

8.

cube   cub

9.

beds   beads

10.

cape   cap

11.

bit   bite

12.

eat   at

▶ Look **at the picture.** Circle **the word that will finish the sentence. Print it on the line.**

1. I sit in my _____.

seal
seed
seat

2. It feels nice to rest my _____.

feet
feel
feed

3. Dean heats up the _____.

met
team
meat

4. Mom piles on more _____.

peak
peas
pens

5. Can I eat a heap of _____?

beds
beans
beads

6. After I eat I brush my _____.

teeth
team
ten

 What food do you like best? Why?

 Help your child make up a story using some of the circled words on the page.

Name_____

> Say the name of each picture. Print the missing vowels on the line. Trace the whole word.

1.

f ___ t

2.

h ___ n s

3.

s ___ l

4.

b ___ d

5.

n ___ t

6.

s ___ t

7.

t ___ m

8.

m ___ t

9.

j ___ p

10.

w ___ b

11.

l ___ f

12.

h ___ l

Circle **the word that will finish the** sentence. Print **it on the line.**

jeans
jeep
1. We rode to Lee's game in the _____. peep

_____ seats
seals
2. We sat in a row with many _____. seems

_____ well
week
3. The Seals beat the Bees last _____. keep

_____ lead
leap
4. The Bees are in the _____. leak

_____ neat
need
5. The Seals _____ to win. seed

_____ tent
tame
6. Will Lee's _____ win the game? team

 Which team do you think will win?

 With your child, make up a silly sentence using some of the circled words.

Name_____

Say **the name of each picture.** Print **the name on the line. In the last box, draw a picture of a long e word.** Print **the word.**

1.

heel

2.

3.

4.

5.

6.

7.

8.

9.

10.

11.

12.

Look at the vowel sound. Color the pictures in each row whose names have that vowel sound.

1. Long a

2. Long i

3. Long u

4. Long o

5. Long e

Review long vowels a, i, u, o, e: Phonemic Awareness

 Ask your child to think of rhyming words for three of the picture names.

Name _____

▶ Blend **the letter sounds together as you say each word. Then** color **the picture it names.**

1. c a n e

2. h o s e

3. t u b

4. s e a t

5. p i n

6. d o g

▶ **Blend** the letter sounds together as you **say** each word.
Print the word on the line. **Draw** a line to the picture it names.

1.

c
ub
_____

2.

m
eat
_____

3.

r
ain
_____

4.

p
ig
_____

5.

m
op
_____

6.

t
ube
_____

Review vowels: Blending phonograms

 Help your child make up silly
rhymes for picture names, such as
Hop on a mop.

Name _____

> Say the name of each picture. Print the missing vowels on the lines. Trace the whole word.

1.

c __ t

2.

t __ r __

3.

f __ __ t

4.

r __ b __

5.

t __ b __

6.

b __ __

7.

d __ m __

8.

h __ __

9.

l __ __ f

10.

c __ k __

11.

s __ __ t

12.

n __ __ l

Read the word in the box. Add an e to make a long vowel word. Write it on the first line. Then change the vowel of the word in the box to make a short vowel word. Write it on the second line.

Long Vowel   **Short Vowel**

	Long Vowel	Short Vowel
1. tap	tape	top
2. pin		
3. cut		
4. hop		
5. not		
6. pan		
7. hid		

HOME Help your child think of sentences using short and long vowel word pairs, such as *I did not get a note.*

Name _____

Phonics & Spelling

Say and spell each long vowel word. Print each word on a line in the box that shows its long vowel sound.

fruit	rain	pie	bean	bike
bone	hay	soap	seal	glue

Long a _____ _____

Long i _____ _____

Long u _____ _____

Long o _____ _____

Long e _____ _____

Review long vowels a, i, u, o, e: Spelling **233**

Phonics & Writing

Write a letter to a friend. Tell about a game, sport, or hobby you like. The words in the box may help you.

kite	rope	feet
bike	flute	day

Dear _____,

_____

_____

_____

_____

_____

Your friend,

_____

_____

234 Review long vowels a, i, u, o, e: Writing

You may want to help your child address an envelope and mail the letter to a friend.

Name _____

No Sleep

One night Mike was fast asleep.

1

Mom closed the window. Good night, Mike! Good night, Bruce!

4

Bruce licked Mike's face. That woke him up.

2

FOLD

Next came a blue jeep. It made a loud BEEP.

3

Name_____

 Say **the name of each picture.** Fill in **the bubble beside the picture name.**

1.
- ○ cake
- ○ rake
- ○ coat
- ○ keep

2.
- ○ mile
- ○ mail
- ○ ruler
- ○ mule

3.
- ○ wave
- ○ vase
- ○ five
- ○ dive

4.
- ○ bone
- ○ cone
- ○ cane
- ○ tune

5.
- ○ jeans
- ○ jeep
- ○ deep
- ○ game

6.
- ○ sail
- ○ seem
- ○ rose
- ○ suit

7.
- ○ tie
- ○ toe
- ○ lie
- ○ tire

8.
- ○ rail
- ○ road
- ○ read
- ○ rain

9.
- ○ bait
- ○ goat
- ○ boat
- ○ toad

10.
- ○ tile
- ○ tube
- ○ tape
- ○ time

11.
- ○ mate
- ○ moat
- ○ boat
- ○ meat

12.
- ○ rope
- ○ soap
- ○ pole
- ○ robe

Circle **the word that will finish the** sentence. Print **it on the line.**

1. Sue had a _____ blue kite.

net
neat

2. The kite did _____ have a tail yet.

not
note

3. Joe _____ up rags to make a tail.

cut
cute

4. Then they sailed the _____.

kit
kite

Can you read each word? Put a ✔ in the box if you can.

☐ long ☐ their ☐ where ☐ want ☐ out ☐ little

☐ your ☐ could ☐ about ☐ two ☐ from ☐ why

☐ they ☐ which ☐ them ☐ were ☐ there ☐ because

Read Aloud

Everybody Eats Bread

People came to America from all over the world. They brought many ways to make bread.

French Americans make long, skinny loaves. The crust is crisp and brown. Mexican Americans wrap a flat bread around beans and meat. Jewish Americans bake bread with eggs and milk. They twist the loaf into a braid.

It does not matter what shape bread is. Every shape tastes good!

What kind of bread do you like best?

Dear Family,

In this unit called "Everybody Eats," your child will learn about words that begin and end with consonant blends and words with **y** as a vowel. Many food names, such as grapes, plum, strawberry, milk, and cherry, begin or end with consonant blends or end with **y** as a vowel. As your child becomes familiar with consonant blends and words with **y** as a vowel, you might try these activities together.

▶ Talk with your child about a favorite food. Have him or her draw a picture of the food. Then, help him or her to write a sentence about the food.

I like to eat fruit.

▶ Read the article on page 239 together. Ask your child to identify words with consonant blends and **y** as a vowel.

▶ Your child might enjoy reading these books with you. Look for them in your local library.

The Giant Carrot by Jan Peck

Blueberries for Sal by Robert McCloskey

Sincerely,

_____

Estimada familia:

En esta unidad, titulada "Todos comemos" ("Everybody Eats"), su hijo/a estudiará palabras en inglés que comienzan y terminan con combinaciones de consonantes y palabras con y como una vocal. Muchos nombres de alimentos, como por ejemplo, grapes (uvas), plum (ciruela), strawberry (fresa), milk (leche) y cherry (cereza), comienzan o terminan con grupos de consonantes o terminan con **y** como una vocal. A medida que su hijo/a se vaya familiarizando con los grupos de consonantes y las palabras con **y** como una vocal, pueden hacer las siguientes actividades juntos.

▶ Conversen con su hijo/a sobre una comida favorita. Pídanle que haga un dibujo de dicha comida y después, con su ayuda, que escriba una oración que describa la comida.

▶ Lean juntos el artículo en la página 239. Pidan a su hijo/a que identifique palabras con combinaciones de consonantes e **y** como una vocal.

▶ Ustedes y su hijo/a disfrutarán leyendo estos libros juntos. Búsquenlos en su biblioteca local.

The Giant Carrot de Jan Peck

Blueberries for Sal de Robert McCloskey

Sinceramente,

_____

Name_____

I love to munch
Fresh fruit for brunch
And have a bunch
Of grapes with lunch.

> Say **the name of the first picture in the row.**
> Circle **each picture in the row whose name begins with the same blend.**

grapes

tree

brush

crib

R blends: Sound to symbol **241**

Say the name of the first picture in the row. Color each picture in the row whose name begins with the same blend.

1. prize

2. frog

3. dress

4. train

5. crab

 HOME Ask your child to say the name of each picture and name the first two letters of each word.

Name_____

> **Say the name of each picture. Circle its name.**

1.

free   tree

2.

trick   brick

3.

prize   cries

4.

frog   frame

5.

crab   crib

6.

drive   dress

7.

braid   bride

8.

grapes   grass

9.

crane   crown

10.

drum   drip

11.

frown   frame

12.

grass   grab

Say the name of each picture. Print **its beginning blend** on the line. Trace **the whole word.**

1.

crab

2.

ain

3.

ide

4.

uit

5.

ick

6.

ess

7.

ize

8.

ane

9.

ee

10.

um

11.

ib

12.

og

 HOME

Point to a picture and ask your child to think of another word that begins with the same sound.

Name _____

Slice the plum.
Place it on a plate.
You take some.
I'll be glad to wait.

Say **the name of the first picture in the row.**
Circle **each picture in the row whose name begins**
with the same blend.

1. plug

2. block

3. club

4. flag

5. glass

L blends: Sound to symbol **245**

Say **the name of each picture.** Circle **its name.**

1. block   flock

2. grape   plate

3. class   glass

4. drag   flag

5. clue   glue

6. plug   plum

7. crack   clock

8. plant   plan

9. flat   float

10. grass   glass

11. club   clap

12. fly   cry

HOME

Play a word game with your child by saying, "I say *fly*, you say fl___." Your child supplies a word with the blend.

Name _____

> Say **the name of each picture.** Print **its beginning blend on the line.** Trace **the whole word.**

1. club

2. ant

3. ag

4. ate

5. ock

6. y

7. at

8. ove

9. ock

10. obe

11. ug

12. ue

Say the name of each picture. **Circle** the word that will finish the sentence. **Print** it on the line.

1. Take a peek into my

_____

- - - - - - - - - - - - - - -

_____.

clap
class
grass

2. Bruce draws a funny

_____

- - - - - - - - - - - - - - -

_____.

clock
clown
frown

3. Fran makes a clock from a paper

_____

- - - - - - - - - - - - - - -

_____.

plate
prank
plum

4. Mr. Glen lets us grow

_____

- - - - - - - - - - - - - - -

_____.

plans
plates
plants

5. We play with clay and

_____

- - - - - - - - - - - - - - -

_____.

braids
drives
blocks

6. We look at the

_____

- - - - - - - - - - - - - - -

_____.

globe
glass
grape

 Would you like to do what Bruce and Fran did in school? Why?

 Point to the words *Bruce, Fran, Glen, grow, play, clay* and ask your child to think of more words that begin with the same sounds.

248 L blends: High-frequency words, critical thinking

Name_____

Spice smells nice,
And tastes good, too.
But too much spice
Can spoil the stew.

▶ Say the name of the first picture in the row. Circle all the pictures in the row whose names begin with the same blend.

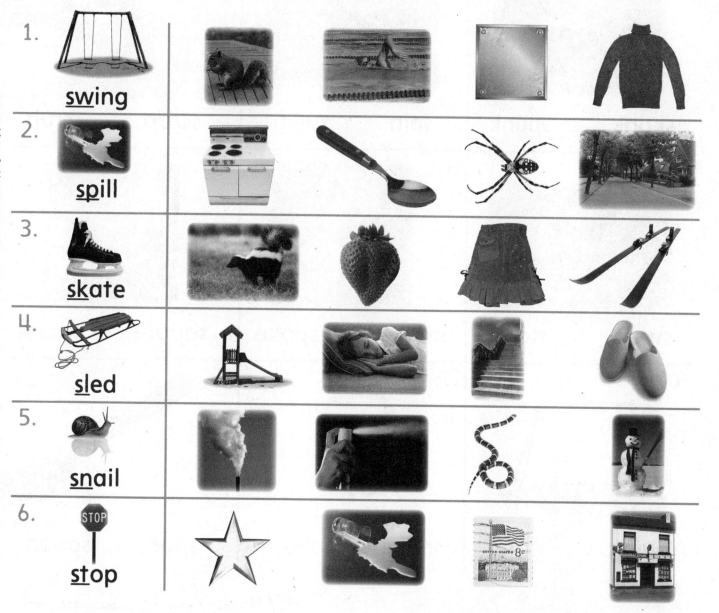

1. swing

2. spill

3. skate

4. sled

5. snail

6. stop

Say the name of each picture. Circle its name.

1.

sled   slide

2.

stops   steps

3.

spill   spade

4.

skunk   spunk

5.

spin   swim

6.

scrap   scrub

7.

sweet   street

8.

smoke   spoke

9.

square   scare

10.

swing   string

11.

snake   skate

12.

spot   spoon

250   S blends: Sound to symbol

HOME Say "s-l, sl." Ask your child to name a word that begins with the sl sound. Repeat for st, sp, sk, sw, sm.

Name _____

Say the name of each picture. Print its beginning blend on the line. Trace the whole word.

1. skate

2. ed

3. ub

4. ar

5. ail

6. op

7. oke

8. irt

9. ill

10. ing

11. are

12. im

Say **the name of the picture.** Circle **the word that will finish the sentence.** Print **it on the line.**

1.

Be sure to _____ and read each rule!

spill
stop
star

2. Take turns on the _____
_____.

slide
sling
slip

3. Do not run near the _____
_____.

sting
swing
swim

4. Please do not pet the _____
_____.

snake
spoke
snail

5. Look before you cross the _____
_____.

steps
street
stamp

6. _____
Always _____ with a pal.

sweep
snake
swim

 TALK About It! **What other safety rules do you know?**

 HOME Help your child to think of new sentences using some of the circled words.

S blends: High-frequency words, critical thinking

Name_____

I'd like to be in a marching band,
With a shiny gold trumpet in my hand.
I'd look my best in my hat and coat,
And I'd never, ever miss a note!

> **Say** the name of the first picture in the row. **Circle** each picture in the row whose name ends with the same blend.

1. jump

2. desk

3. sink

4. list

5. hand

Say the name of each picture. Print **its ending blend** on the line. Trace **the whole word.**

1.

trunk

2.

la

3.

de

4.

mi

5.

li

6.

wi

7.

ne

8.

si

9.

ma

10.

be

11.

ju

12.

ha

 HOME

Ask your child to point to a picture, name a word that rhymes, and then name the letters in the final blend.

254   Final blends: Spelling

Name_____

> **Blend** the letter sounds together as you say each word. **Color** the picture it names.

1.

sl
e
d

2.

cr
i
b

3.

pl
u
g

4.

fl
a
g

5.

dr
u
m

Blend the letter sounds together as you say each word. Then print the word on the line. Draw a line to the picture it names.

1. s i nk

2. l i st

3. m i lk

4. g i ft

5. j u mp

6. d e sk

Point to a word. Ask your child to name the final blend, then say a word with the same final blend.

Name _____

Read **the story. Then, use words from** the story to finish **the sentences.**

Fred's Bread

Fred made some bread.
He mixed flour, water,
and too much yeast.
The bread grew and grew.
Now Fred had too much bread!
He asked his friends to stop by.
They sliced the soft bread and made toast.
Then they spread jam on the toast.
They had a feast!

_____

1. Fred made some _____.

2. Fred asked his friends to _____ by.

3. He and his friends had a _____.

Why did Fred end up with so much bread?

Review consonant blends: Reading, critical thinking **257**

Add the word part to each of the blends in the boxes. Say the word. If it is a real word, write it on the line.

| tr | sm | br | cl | sl |

ick

1. _____
2. _____
3. _____
4. _____

| pl | gr | gl | cl | st |

ay

5. _____
6. _____
7. _____
8. _____

Write a sentence using two of the words you made.

_____
_____
_____

HOME Ask your child to make up a sentence using two more of the words he or she wrote.

Name _____

Won't you try my berry pie?
The crust is flaky, my, oh my.
Come on, have some.
Don't be shy.
If you won't try it, I may cry!

▶ Say the name of the picture. Circle the words in the boxes with the same sound of **y** as the picture name. Then, circle the pictures whose names have the vowel sound of **y**.

1.

by	lazy	yellow	dry	yet
my	sky	yoke	cry	yarn

2.

yes	fry	you	yard	funny
yellow	puppy	sly	yell	windy

3.

fly	candy	yams	lady	penny
pry	fairy	baby	try	pony

► **Say the name of each picture. Circle its name.**

1.

puppy   buggy

2.

fry   fly

3.

lady   baby

4.

funny   penny

5.

pony   penny

6.

cry   try

7.

spy   sky

8.

fifty   twenty

9.

sly   fry

 HOME

Point to each picture and help your child think of a word or name that rhymes, such as *puppy-guppy*.

Name_____

▶ Say the name of each picture. Circle the word that will finish the sentence. Print it on the line.

1. Wendy can not ride a

_____

- - - - - - - - - - - - -

_____

bony
pony
penny

2. She is too small to feed a

_____

- - - - - - - - - - - - -

_____

puffy
poppy
puppy

3. She can not draw the

_____

- - - - - - - - - - - - -

_____

sky
sly
spy

4. Mom will not let her eat

_____

- - - - - - - - - - - - -

_____

sandy
candy
funny

5. I feel sad if she starts to

_____

- - - - - - - - - - - - -

_____

my
cry
try

6. Wendy is only a

_____

- - - - - - - - - - - - -

_____

bunny
baby
buggy

 TALK About It! **What can a baby do?**

Y as a vowel: High-frequency words, critical thinking **261**

Say the name of each picture. Print the picture name on the line. In the last box, draw a picture of a word in which y is a vowel. Write the word.

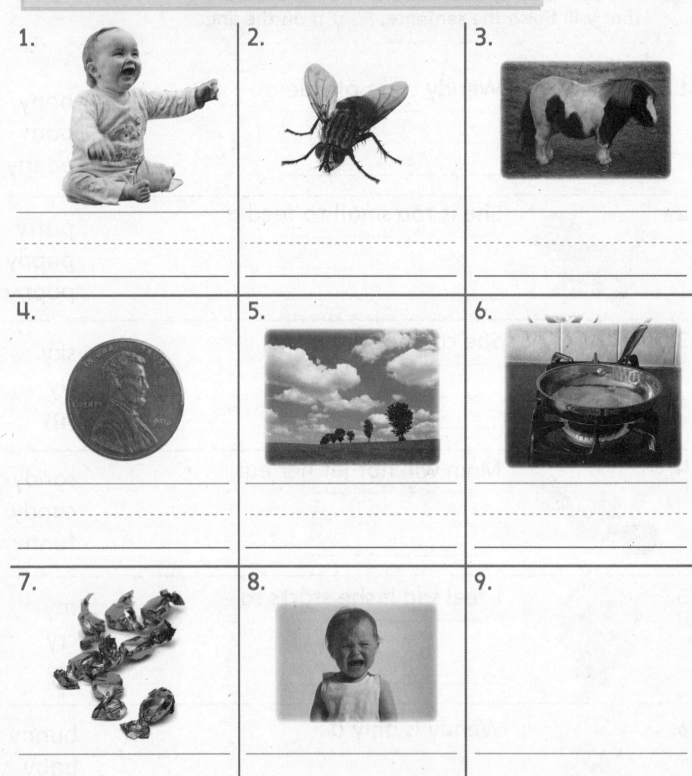

1. _____

2. _____

3. _____

4. _____

5. _____

6. _____

7. _____

8. _____

9. _____

 Ask your child to say the name of his or her picture and spell the word.

Name_____

Phonics & Spelling

Read the sentences. **Use** the mixed-up letters to make a word from the box. **Print** the word on the line to finish the sentence.

grapes   try   bread   fresh   smell

1. "The fruit looks _____," Clare said.   **s h r e f**

2. "Let us buy some _____," said Greg.   **a r p e g s**

3. "I will _____ to find green ones."   **r t y**

4. "Just _____ the plums!" Clare said.   **e l l s m**

5. "Now all we need is _____."   **e a d b r**

How do you think the plums smell?

Review consonant blends and y as a vowel:
Words in context, critical thinking   **263**

Write a shopping list for your family's next trip to the store. List things to buy. Look at the words in the box for help.

bread	drink	sweet	fruit
plums	grapes	milk	berry

SHOPPING LIST

HOME Talk with your child about what items could be added to the list.

Name _____

PIZZA FEAST

Did you ever try to make a pizza?
First, you make the crust.

1

- FOLD - - - - - - - - - -

Bake the pizza till it is crisp. Then,
put it on a plate. It will taste great!

4

Press the crust in a pan. Make it round and flat.

2

Spread the sauce and cheese all over.

3

FOLD

Say the name of each picture. Fill in the bubble beside the picture name.

1.
○ trip
○ prize
○ train
○ drain

2.
○ snail
○ snake
○ skate
○ string

3.
○ clock
○ braid
○ blouse
○ block

4.
○ crab
○ grab
○ club
○ crib

5.
○ flag
○ glass
○ flat
○ blank

6.
○ green
○ dress
○ drum
○ desk

7.
○ deck
○ drive
○ desk
○ jump

8.
○ clap
○ plant
○ plug
○ plate

9.
○ stamp
○ steps
○ stop
○ spill

10.
○ glue
○ globe
○ drive
○ glove

11.
○ frame
○ lamp
○ fly
○ frog

12.
○ glass
○ spot
○ spoon
○ smoke

Circle **the word that will finish each** sentence. Print **it on the line.**

1. _____ the day with a good meal.

Stop
Start
Star

2. Corn _____ and milk are great.

flags
frames
flakes

3. _____ adding some fruit.

Fry
Try
Why

4. _____ a glass of juice.

Drink
Trunk
Dress

5. Some _____ is good, too.

float
test
toast

6. Stay away from _____ things.

sweet
smoke
square

Read Aloud

Let it Snow!

In a blizzard, the wind blows very hard. Snow falls faster and very heavily. The temperature is close to zero. The heavy snow and blowing wind make it hard to see.

Once, a big blizzard hit Chicago. Schools and offices were closed for days. There was so much snow that some of it was sent by train to Florida. Children in Florida had never seen snow!

How do you find out what the weather will be each day?

Dear Family,

In this unit, "Whatever the Weather," your child will learn about contractions, words ending with **ed** and **ing,** and consonant digraphs. A consonant digraph is formed with two letters that stand for one sound. For example, the **sh** in sheep and the **th** in thermometer are digraphs. As your child becomes familiar with these concepts, you might try these activities together.

▶ Help your child to create a weather chart. For each day of the week, he or she can draw a picture of that day's weather. At the end of the week, ask your child to tell you what the weather was each day.

▶ With your child, read the article on page 269. Help him or her to identify the words with consonant digraphs and contractions and words that end in **ed** or **ing.**

▶ Your child might enjoy reading these books with you. Look for them in your local library.

The Snowy Day
by Ezra Jack Keats

Let's Count the Raindrops
by Fumi Kosaka

Sincerely,

_____

Estimada familia:

En esta unidad, titulada "Pronósticos del tiempo" ("Whatever the Weather"), su hijo/a estudiará en inglés contracciones, palabras que terminan en **ed** y en **ing** y digramas de consonantes. Un digrama de consonantes está formado por dos letras que representan un sonido. Por ejemplo, la **sh** en sheep (oveja) y la **th** en thermometer (termómetro) son digramas. A medida que su hijo/a se vaya familiarizando con estos conceptos, pueden hacer las siguientes actividades juntos.

▶ Ayuden a su hijo/a a crear un mapa meteorológico. Para cada día de la semana, su hijo/a puede hacer un dibujo sobre el tiempo que hubo ese día. Al final de la semana, pídanle que les explique cuál fue el tiempo en cada día.

▶ Lean juntos el artículo en la página 269. Ayuden a su hijo/a a identificar las palabras con contracciones, los digramas de consonantes y las palabras que terminan en **ed** o en **ing.**

▶ Ustedes y su hijo/a disfrutarán leyendo estos libros juntos. Búsquenlos en su biblioteca local.

The Snowy Day de Ezra Jack Keats

Let's Count the Raindrops de Fumi Kosaka

Sinceramente,

_____

Name_____

It rained and poured all week.
Now it's raining again.
The puddles are growing so big!
I'm jumping and playing in them.

 Say the name of each picture. Print the ending you see in the corner of the box to finish its name. Trace the whole word.

1. ed

spilled

2. ed

melt

3. ing

eat

4. ing

rain

5. ed

boil

6. ing

fish

7. ed

row

8. ed

peel

9. ing

cry

Read the word below each picture. Each picture name has a base word and an ending. Trace the circle around the base word. Then, read the words beside each picture. Circle each base word.

1.

jumped

asked	yelled	fixed	played
mixed	rocked	bumped	rained

2.

reading

going	telling	sailing	mixing
asking	waiting	resting	boating

3.

melted

waited	seated	heated	landed
mailed	loaded	floated	ended

4.

cooking

rowing	crying	flying	fishing
picking	saying	eating	melting

HOME With your child, hunt for words with endings in favorite storybooks.

Name_____

▶ Circle **the word that will finish the sentence. Print it on the line.**

_____

1. We were _____ to eat.

waiting
waited

_____

2. Dad was _____ the ham.

cooking
cooked

_____

3. Mom was _____ for help.

asking
asked

_____

4. She and I _____ the baby.

dressing
dressed

_____

5. Sandy _____ the fruit.

peeling
peeled

_____

6. I _____ the most!

helping
helped

How does this family help each other?

Inflectional endings -ed and -ing:
High-frequency words, critical thinking   **273**

Circle **the word that will finish the sentence.**
Print it on the line.

1. Dad was _____ fishing.	go going
2. I _____ him to take me to Mary's home.	asking asked
3. We were _____ a ball to each other.	kicked kicking
4. Then we _____ to get wet.	started starting
5. It was _____ cats and dogs.	rain raining
6. We _____ for the rain to stop.	waiting waited
7. Then we _____ on Mary's swing set.	played playing

 What does "raining
cats and dogs" mean?

Inflectional endings -ed and -ing:
274 High-frequency words, critical thinking

 Using words with endings, take turns
telling what you did today.

Name_____

My soft mittens are thick, not thin.
My fingers and thumbs stay warm in them.
When the thermometer says thirty-three,
Outside with my mittens is where I'll be.

▶ Thumb **begins with the sound of th.** Circle **each
picture whose name begins with the sound of th.**

1.

2.

3

3.

2

4.

5.

6.

7.

30

8.

9.

10.

11.

12.

13

Say the name of each picture. Print **th** or **t** to finish each word. Trace the whole word.

1. thick

2. in

3. ire

4. ink

5. irty

6. ie

7. iger

8. ape

9. ree

10. umb

11. orn

12. en

Help your child to make up a sentence using words with *t* and *th*, such as *Thirty tigers had thick tails.*

Name_____

The wind whines and whistles.
It whips through the tree.
It whirls around wildly,
And takes my white cap from me!

▶ White **begins with the sound of wh.** Circle each
picture whose name begins with the sound of **wh.**

1.

2.

3.

4.

5.

6.

7.

8.

9.

10.

11.

12.

Consonant digraph wh: Phonemic awareness   **277**

Say the name of each picture.
Print **wh** or **th** to finish each word.
Trace the whole word.

1.

_ _ _ eel

2.

_ _ _ umb

3.

_ _ _ ick

4.

_ _ _ orn

5.

_ _ _ eat

6.

_ _ _ ink

7.

_ _ _ ale

8.

_ _ _ in

9.

_ _ _ ite

10.

_ _ _ ree

11.

_ _ _ read

12.

_ _ _ istle

 HOME

Ask your child: *What comes after two and before four?* Take turns making up riddles for other picture names.

Name _____

Shannon is in the sunlight.
What does she see?
A shiny, shimmering shadow.
She says, "You can't catch me!"

▶ Shadow **begins with the sound of sh.**
Circle each picture whose name begins
with the sound of sh.

1.

2.

3.

4.

5.

6.

7.

8.

9.

10.

11.

12.

Say the name of each picture.
Print **sh** or **s** to finish each word.
Trace the whole word.

1. _____ ell

2. _____ ail

3. _____ ade

4. _____ ix

5. _____ oe

6. _____ elf

7. _____ ip

8. _____ eep

9. _____ eat

10. _____ irt

11. _____ ock

12. _____ out

 Ask your child to make up sentences using some of the words on the page.

Name_____

Outside it was chilly.
Chen's pets chose to stay indoors.
Chen sat in a chair with Lily,
While Chip chased yarn on the floor.

> **Chair begins with the sound of ch. Circle each picture whose name begins with the sound of ch.**

1.

2.

3.

4.

5.

6.

7.

8.

9.

10.

11.

12.

Say the name of each picture. Print **ch** or **c** to finish each word. Trace the whole word.

1.

_ _ _ _ in

2.

_ _ _ _ eck

3.

_ _ _ _ oat

4.

_ _ _ _ eese

5.

_ _ _ _ ube

6.

_ _ _ _ ick

7.

_ _ _ _ alk

8.

_ _ _ _ at

9.

_ _ _ _ ain

10.

_ _ _ _ erry

11.

_ _ _ _ ow

12.

_ _ _ _ air

282 Discriminating between ch and c: Spelling

 HOME

Ask your child to identify common household items whose names begin with *ch* or *c*, such as *chair* and *comb*.

Name _____

Knock, knock, knock.
Who's knocking at the door?
We know who it is—
The wind, and nothing more!

> **Knock** begins with the letters **kn.** You only hear the sound of **n.** Say the name of each picture. Trace the whole word. Then, circle the pictures whose names begin with **kn.**

1. knee

2. think

3. knot

4. knob

5. knife

6. whale

7. chin

8. knock

9. knit

Circle the sentence that tells about the picture.

1.

   The tire is black and white.

   Chad tied a knot in the rope.

2.

   Randy did not skin his knee.

   Kelly kneels down on the mat.

3.

   Did you hear a knock at the door?

   Did Nick knock over the vase?

4.

   I fed the bread to the chicks.

   I used a knife to slice the cheese.

5.

   Chuck knows where his watch is.

   Kate turned the knob to the left.

6.

   Susan knits a sweater for her sister.

   Jenny ties a knot with her shoe strings.

7.

   The knight does not ride a horse.

   The knight rides a horse with spots.

HOME Ask your child to point to and read each *kn* word.

Name_____

> Circle **the word that will finish the sentence.** Print **it on the line.**

1. Chuck _____ about a sunny beach.

knows
knob
knock

2. We catch the bus at _____.

thick
three
thorn

3. Beth puts a _____ sheet down.

white
wheat
whip

4. Chuck finds _____ in the sand.

sheets
shades
shells

5. I _____ Beth a new game.

teach
reach
cheat

6. Then we sit and look at the _____.

shape
ships
shake

What else can people do at the beach?

Review consonant digraphs:
High-frequency words, critical thinking   **285**

Read **each clue.** Print **the answer to each riddle on the line.** Use **the cloud pictures if you need help.**

three	sheep	wheel	cherry
ship	chick	whale	knife

1. My hair is called wool.
   I can be white, brown, or black.

   I am a _____.

2. I hatch out of an egg.
   My mother is a hen.

   I am a _____.

3. I live in the sea.
   I am much bigger than a fish.

   I am a _____.

4. I sail across the sea.
   People ride in me.

   I am a _____.

5. I come after two
   and before four.

   I am _____.

6. I am round. I help
   cars and bikes go.

   I am a _____.

7. I am round and red.
   I am good to eat.

   I am a _____.

8. I am very sharp. People
   use me to cut things.

   I am a _____.

Review consonant digraphs:
High-frequency words

Ask your child to read the riddles to you so you can guess the answers.

Name_____

▶ **Blend** the letter sounds together as you say each word. **Print** the word on the line. **Draw** a line to the picture it names.

1.
ch
i n

2.
th
i n k

3.
kn
o b

4.
sh
e l f

5.
wh
e a t

6.
kn
e e

Look at the picture. Then follow the directions.

1. Color the ship black.
2. Circle the shell on the beach.
3. Write a three on the flag.
4. Color the wheel brown.
5. Color the thick rope yellow.
6. Draw a whale in the water.
7. Draw a box around each knot.
8. Color the sky blue but keep the cloud white.

With your child, make up a story to go with the picture.

Name_____

Read **the story.** Use **words in which two letters stand for one beginning sound and words with endings to finish the sentences.**

Looking for Chuck

Where was Chuck?
Shari and Shane looked all over.
They knew Chuck did not like storms.
Now thunder was booming.
Lightning flashed.
Chuck was hiding.
After a while Shari sat down.
She said, "I give up."
Just then Shane said, "There's Chuck!
He's chewing his toy under your chair!"

_____

1. _____ was Chuck?

_____

2. _____ was booming.

_____

3. Chuck was _____ his toy.

Why was Chuck hiding?

Add **the word part to each of the letter pairs in the boxes.** Say **the word. If it is a real word,** write **it on the line.**

| th | ch | kn | wh | sh |

in

1. _____

2. _____

3. _____

| th | ch | wh | sh | kn |

ip

4. _____

5. _____

6. _____

▶ Write **a sentence using two of the words you made.**

_____

_____

_____

HOME Ask your child to think of more words that begin with *th, wh, sh, ch,* and *kn.*

Name _____

CLOUDS

Clouds come in many shapes and colors. Did you know they can tell you about the weather?

1

----------FOLD----------

Cumulus Clouds

These white clouds mean good weather, too. It is fun to watch them change their shapes.

4

Cumulonimbus Clouds

These clouds are showing that bad weather is near. Rain and thunder will come soon.

2

---FOLD---

Cirrus Clouds

These thin clouds are made of ice. They tell us that the weather will be good.

3

Name_____

They'll slide down the hill.
They will go very fast.
I'll slide down, too.
I will be the last.

I will = I'll
he will = he'll

you will = you'll
she will = she'll
it will = it'll

they will = they'll
we will = we'll

 They'll is a short way to say **they will.** Read each sentence. Circle the short way to write the underlined words.

1. It will be fun to go for a ride on a sled.	You'll It'll
2. I will get on the sled.	We'll I'll
3. You will get on the sled with me.	You'll She'll
4. They will all get on the sled, too.	They'll It'll
5. Oh, no! Get off or we will fall!	he'll we'll

 TALK About It

What are some other things to do outside when the weather is cold?

She's **is a short way to say** she is. **Look at each picture.**
Read the sentence. Print the short way to write the
<u>**underlined words.**</u> **Use the words in the box to help you.**

she is = she's   it is = it's   he is = he's

1. <u>It is</u> a nice day to play in the park.

_____

- - - - - - - - - - - - - - - -

_____ a nice day to play in the park.

2. <u>He is</u> going down the slide.

_____

- - - - - - - - - - - - - - - -

_____ going down the slide.

3. <u>She is</u> having fun in the water.

_____

- - - - - - - - - - - - - - - -

_____ having fun in the water.

4. <u>He is</u> playing on the swings.

_____

- - - - - - - - - - - - - - - -

_____ playing on the swings.

5. <u>It is</u> full of things to do!

_____

- - - - - - - - - - - - - - - -

_____ full of things to do!

 TALK **What else can you do**
About It **at the park?**

 HOME Ask your child what words form the
contractions *they'll*, *we'll*, and *you'll*.

Contractions with is: Words in context, critical thinking

Name _____

I'm is a short way to say **I am.** Look at each picture.
Read the sentence. Print the short way to write the
<u>underlined words.</u> Use the words in the box to help you.

> I am = I'm   we are = we're
> you are = you're   they are = they're

1. <u>You are</u> going to the zoo.

_____

- - - - - - - - - - - - - - - -

_____ going to the zoo.

2. <u>I am</u> going with you.

_____

- - - - - - - - - - - - - - - -

_____ going with you.

3. <u>We are</u> going to see the seals.

_____

- - - - - - - - - - - - - - - -

_____ going to see the seals.

4. <u>They are</u> fun, and the cubs are, too.

_____

- - - - - - - - - - - - - - - -

_____ fun, and the cubs are, too.

5. I think <u>we are</u> going to love the zoo!

_____

- - - - - - - - - - - - - - - -

I think _____ going to love the zoo!

 **What other animals
can you see at the zoo?**

Contractions with am and are:
Words in context, critical thinking **295**

Can't **is a short way to say can not.** Read the sentences. Circle **the short way to write the <u>underlined words</u>.** Use **the words in the box to help you.**

can not = can't   does not = doesn't

will not = won't   is not = isn't

1. Wags <u>is not</u> clean. He is a muddy mess!	can't doesn't isn't
2. Mom says he needs a bath. Wags just <u>will not</u> get into the tub.	won't isn't doesn't
3. Wags <u>does not</u> like baths. He runs away.	isn't can't doesn't
4. I <u>can not</u> catch him. Mom will help me.	can't doesn't won't
5. Wags <u>is not</u> muddy now. I am the one who needs a bath!	isn't can't doesn't

TALK About It

Who needs a bath now and why?

HOME

Using the contractions, take turns making up other sentences about Wags.

Name _____

> **Circle the sentence that tells about the picture.**

1.

   I'll eat the hot dog.

   I'm going to read the book.

2.

   It's in the bag.

   She'll sleep in the tent.

3.

   We won't go on the ride.

   We're on the ride.

4.

   She's going to play on the swing.

   They're going to like my painting.

5.

   You're going to rake the yard.

   We'll drive up to the lake.

6.

   I can't skate very well on the ice.

   He doesn't like ice cream on his cake.

Fill in the bubble beside the sentence that tells about the picture.

1. ○ It's a dog.
   ○ It can't be a dog.
   ○ They're dogs.

2. ○ He's on a bike.
   ○ She's in a jet.
   ○ I'm on the bus.

3. ○ It won't rain today.
   ○ It'll rain all day.
   ○ I'll play in the rain.

4. HOT DOGS 50¢
   ○ We don't like bugs.
   ○ She'll eat a hot dog.
   ○ We're eating the fruit.

5. ○ They'll go for a ride.
   ○ We'll go for a swim.
   ○ You're up a tree.

6. ○ She can't find her shoes.
   ○ He doesn't want to ride his bike.
   ○ She's trying to catch a fish.

HOME Ask your child to use contractions such as *I'll, I'm,* and *won't* to tell about himself or herself.

Name _____

Say and spell the words below. Print the words on the lines where they belong.

fishing	can't	melted	I'm	peeled	ship
think	knot	chin	whale	rowing	spilled

Words that have **ed** endings

1. _____ 2. _____ 3. _____

Words that take the place of two small words

4. _____ 5. _____

Words whose beginning sound is made up of two letters

6. _____ 7. _____ 8. _____

9. _____ 10. _____

Words that have **ing** endings

11. _____ 12. _____

Phonics & Writing

What kind of weather do you like best? Write a description of your favorite kind of weather. Use describing words to tell about what you see, hear, or feel. The words in the box may help you.

know	I'm	playing	walking
rained	what	that	it's

_____

- - - - - - - - - - - - - - - - - - - -

_____

- - - - - - - - - - - - - - - - - - - -

_____

- - - - - - - - - - - - - - - - - - - -

_____

- - - - - - - - - - - - - - - - - - - -

_____

- - - - - - - - - - - - - - - - - - - -

_____

- - - - - - - - - - - - - - - - - - - -

_____

Review endings, digraphs, contractions: Writing

HOME Ask your child to forecast tomorrow's weather.

Name _____

It's Raining

Chad and Trina looked out. "It's raining," Trina said. "We can't play out there."

1

"It isn't raining," said Trina. "It's Dad! He's making it rain!"

4

Review endings, digraphs, contractions: Take-home book   **301**

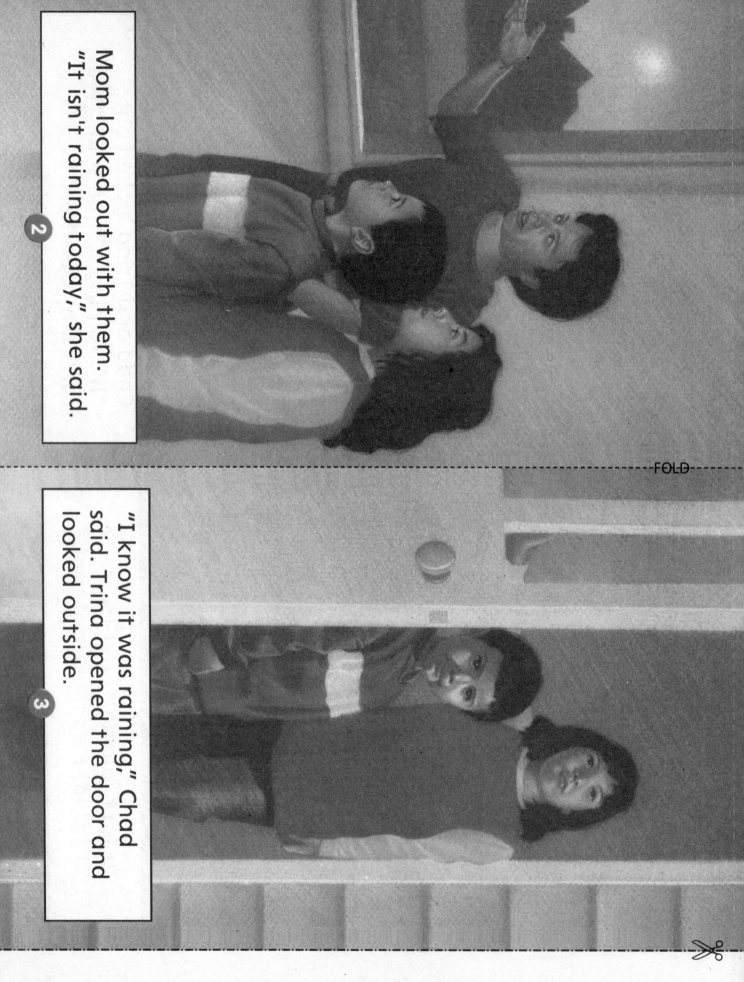

Mom looked out with them. "It isn't raining today," she said.

2

"I know it was raining," Chad said. Trina opened the door and looked outside.

3

FOLD

Name _____

Say the name of each picture. Fill in the bubble beside the picture name.

1.

○ knee
○ knob
○ knife

2.

○ wheel
○ whip
○ white

3.

○ chain
○ thin
○ chin

4.

○ sheep
○ ship
○ chip

5.

○ thin
○ cherry
○ three

6.

○ knit
○ knot
○ knock

7.

○ chair
○ shame
○ chat

8.

○ while
○ throat
○ whale

9.

○ throne
○ thumb
○ shade

> Look **at the picture.** Circle **the word that will finish the sentence.** Print **it on the line.**

1.

How deep do you _____ it is?

think
knew
chase

2.

She's _____ to find out.

rowing
spilled
trying

3.

It's up to his _____!

knot
chin
whale

4.

She _____ get it out.

isn't
don't
can't

5.

_____ happy that it snowed.

They're
I'll
It's

6.

The snow has all _____!

peeled
spilled
melted

PEARSON
Phonics
LEVEL A Elwell • Murray • Kucia

ILLUSTRATIONS: Page 249, Anthony Accardo. 4, 215, 277: Elizabeth Allen. 156: Bob Berry. 274: Gary Bialke. 172: Chi Chung. 99: Genevieve Claire. 1, 7, 9, 53, 63, 122: Lynn Cravath. 86, 165, 208: Molly Delaney. 1, 83, 296: Chris Demarest. 289: Karen Dugan. 19, 21, 49, 297, 298: Julie Durrell. 202, 295: Len Ebert. 145: Alan Eitzen. 284, 304: Kate Flanagan. 35, 37: Brian Floca. 259: Toni Goffe. 113: Linda Graves. 5: Shelly Hehenberger. 54, 64, 184, 245, 293: Meryl Henderson. 17, 285: Dennis Hockerman. 159: Joan Holub. 16, 40, 42, 55, 65, 152, 174, 190: Ann Iosa. 29, 45, 92, 163, 226, 273: Meredith Johnson. 261: Wallace Keller. 216, 283: Anne Kennedy. 3, 7, 109, 257: Jeff Le Van. 50, 164, 217: Anni Matsick 11: ErinMauterer. 188, 224, 248: Kathleen McCarthy. 106, 136: Patrick Merrel. 144: Susan Miller. 90: Cheryl Kirk Noll 193: Christina Ong. 240: Pearson learning. 220, 275: Mick Reid. 17, 19, 108, 129, 135, 279: Francesc Rovira. 43, 49: Ellen Sasaki. 299: Stacey Schuett. 93: Janet Skiles. 138: Susan Spellman. 177, 178: Nicole Tadgell. 76, 233: Terry Taylor. 99: Lynn Titleman. 13, 150, 211: George Ulrich. 181, 183, 197, 241, 271, 281: Gary Undercuffler. 27: Baker Vail. 102: Teri Weidner 286: Thor Wickstrom. 301, 302: Fred Willingham. 158, 206, 252: Amy Wummer. 272: Lane Yerkrs.

ACKNOWLEDGMENTS: "Play" by Frank Asch from Country Pie by Frank Asch. Copyright 1979 by Frank Asch. Greenwillow Books (A division of Willium Morrow & Co.)

NOTE: Every effort has been made to locate the copyright owner of material reprinted in this book. Omissions brought to our attention will be corrected in subsequent printings.

PHOTOGRAPHS: Cover: m. © Silver/Fotolia, inset. © Ruth Black/Fotolia. Page 6: B-tl. © Carl Subick/Fotolia, B-tr. © Hemera Technologies/Thinkstock, B-bl. © Henk Bentlage/Fotolia, B-bm. © PhotoZA/Fotolia, C-tl. © Africa Studio/Fotolia, C-tr. © Luchshen/Fotolia, C-m. © David De Lossy/Thinkstock, C-bl. © Vasiliy Koval/Fotolia, C-br. © Route66Photography/Fotolia. 8: tm. © Abderit99/Fotolia, mr. © Lisa Turay/Fotolia, tl. © Hemera Technologies/ Thinkstock, tr. © Sergik/Fotolia, ml. © James Steidl/Fotolia, m. © fotogal/Fotolia, bl. © Cphoto/Fotolia, bm. © aris sanjaya/Fotolia, br. © Stockbyte/ Thinkstock. 9: mr. © drx/Fotolia, tml. © Stockbyte/Thinkstock, tmr. © Thinkstock, ml. © Hemera Technologies/Thinkstock, mml. © Marie-Thérèse GUIHAL/Fotolia, mmr. © Studio Gi/Fotolia, bl. © Melking/Fotolia, bmr. © Borys Shevchuk/Fotolia, br. © Thomas Northcut/Thinkstock, tl. © Elaine Barker/Fotolia, tr. © Iznogood/Fotolia, bml. © Iznogood/Fotolia. 10: bl. © Jagi/Fotolia, mbr. © Linous/Fotolia, tm. © Lilyana Vynogradova/Fotolia, tl. © Marie-Thérèse GUIHAL/Fotolia, mtm. © Sotern/Fotolia, mtr. © Borys Shevchuk/Fotolia, mbl. © Thomas Northcut/Thinkstock, mbm. © Vasiliy Koval/Fotolia, bm. © Melking/Fotolia, br. © Ilandrea/Fotolia, tr. © Elaine Barker/Fotolia, mtl. © Iznogood/Fotolia. 11: tl. © Picture Partners/Fotolia, mmr. © Abderit99/Fotolia, tml. © Melking/Fotolia, tmr. © a4stockphotos/Fotolia, mml. © Hemera Technologies/Thinkstock, mml. © Close Encounters/ Fotolia, mr. © Jupiterimages/Thinkstock, bmr. © Iosif Szasz-Fabian/Fotolia, br. © RoJo Images/Fotolia, tr. © Iznogood/Fotolia, bl. © Iznogood/ Fotolia, bml. © auris/Fotolia. 12: mbr. © Lisa Turay/Fotolia, mtl. © Lilyana Vynogradova/Fotolia, tl. © Picture Partners/Fotolia, tm. © Iosif Szasz-Fabian/Fotolia, tr. © Marie-Thérèse GUIHAL/Fotolia, mtm. © Jupiterimages/Thinkstock, mtr. © Thinkstock, mbm. © Marsel/Fotolia, bl. © Gordan Gledec/Fotolia, bm. © a4stockphotos/Fotolia, mbl. © Iznogood/Fotolia, br. © Elaine Barker/Fotolia. 13: bl. © Alexford/Fotolia, tml. © Yxowert/Fotolia, tr. © Abderit99/Fotolia, ml. © Laurent Renault/Fotolia, tl. © Carl SubickFotolia, tmr. © Hemera Technologies/Thinkstock, mml. © Michael Kempf/Fotolia, mmr. © Rtimages/Fotolia, mr. © Hemera Technologies/Thinkstock, bml. © Marie-Thérèse GUIHAL/Fotolia, bmr. © Thinkstock, br. © Iosif Szasz-Fabian/Fotolia. 14: tm. © Alexford/Fotolia, br. © Yxowert/Fotolia, tl. © Rtimages/Fotolia, tr. © Carl SubickFotolia, mtl. © Elnur/Fotolia, mtm. © Borys Shevchuk/Fotolia, mtr. © Stockbyte/Thinkstock, mbl. © Hemera Technologies/Thinkstock, mbr. © Michael Kempf/Fotolia, bl. © Thinkstock, bm. © a4stockphotos/Fotolia, mbm. © Elaine Barker/Fotolia. 15: mml. © Hemera Technologies/Thinkstock, tl. © Carl SubickFotolia, tml. © Sneekerp/Fotolia, tmr. © Michael Kempf/Fotolia, tr. © Stockbyte/Thinkstock, ml. © Getty Images/Jupiterimages/ Thinkstock, mmr. © Marie-Thérèse GUIHAL/Fotolia, mr. © Hemera Technologies/Thinkstock, bl. © Stockbyte/Thinkstock, bml. © Iznogood/Fotolia, bmr. © Iznogood/Fotolia, br. © Hellen/Fotolia. 16: 3-tr. © Jupiterimages/Thinkstock, 3-tm. © Lisa/Turay/Fotolia, 3-tl. © Tschmittjohn/Fotolia, 3-bm. © Linous/Fotolia, 1-tl. © Marsel/Fotolia, 1-tm. © Hemera Technologies/Thinkstock, 1-tr. © Kasoga/Fotolia, 1-ml. © Melking/Fotolia, 1-mr. © Thomas Northcut/Thinkstock, 1-bl. © Lev Olkha/Fotolia, 1-bm. © Paul Moore/Fotolia, 1-br. © Rtimages/Fotolia, 2-tl. © Stockbyte/Thinkstock, 2-tm. © Getty Images/Jupiterimages/Thinkstock, 2-tr. © Borys Shevchuk/Fotolia, 2-ml. © Ionescu Bogdan/Fotolia, 2-m. © Picture Partners/Fotolia, 2-mr. © Stockbyte/Thinkstock, 2-br. © Stockbyte/Thinkstock, 3-ml. © Jupiterimages/Thinkstock, 3-m. © Thinkstock, 3-bl. © Hemera Technologies/ Thinkstock, 3-br. © Studio Gi/Fotolia, 1-m. © Elaine Barker/Fotolia, 2-bl. © Iznogood/Fotolia, 2-bm. © Iznogood/Fotolia, 3-mr. © Iznogood/Fotolia. 17: br. © Hemera Technologies/Thinkstock, tl. © Sergik/Fotolia, bm. © Thomas Northcut/Thinkstock, tm. © auris/Fotolia, tr. © Iznogood/Fotolia, bl. © Elaine Barker/Fotolia. 18: br. © Gravicapa/Fotolia, mbm. © Hemera Technologies/Thinkstock, tl. © Sergik/Fotolia, tm. © Getty Images/Polka Dot RF/Thinkstock, mtl. © Getty Images/Jupiterimages/Thinkstock, mtm. © Michael Gray/Fotolia, mtr. © Olga Sapegina/Fotolia, mbl. © Thomas Northcut/Thinkstock, mbr. © Gordan Gledec/Fotolia, bl. © Iosif Szasz-Fabian/Fotolia, bm. © Valua Vitaly/Fotolia, tr. © auris/Fotolia. 19: bmr. © Yxowert/Fotolia, tr. © Emilia Stasiak/Fotolia, bml. © Getty Images/Hemera Technologies/Thinkstock, tl. © Olga Sapegina/Fotolia, tml. © Valua Vitaly/Fotolia, tmr. © Jupiterimages/Thinkstock, ml. © Studio Gi/Fotolia, mml. © Getty Images/ Polka Dot RF/Thinkstock, mmr. © Zedcor Wholly Owned/Thinkstock, mr. © Iryna Volina/Fotolia, bl. © Ablestock.com/Thinkstock, br. © Jiri Hera/Fotolia. 20: mbl. © Emilia Stasiak/Fotolia, tl. © Getty Images/Hemera Technologies/Thinkstock, tm. © Olga Sapegina/Fotolia, tr. © Ana Vasileva/Fotolia, mtl. © Carl SubickFotolia, mtr. © Getty Images/ Polka Dot RF/Thinkstock, mbm. © Iryna Volina/Fotolia, mbr. © Jiri Hera/Fotolia, bl. © Picture Partners/Fotolia, br. © Ernst Fretz/Fotolia, mtm. © Iznogood/Fotolia, bm. © auris/Fotolia, mbr. © auris/Fotolia. 21: bl. © George Doyle/Thinkstock, br. © Kitch Bain/Fotolia, tl. © Iosif Szasz-Fabian/ Fotolia, tm. © James Steidl/Fotolia, tr. © Gordan Gledec/Fotolia, bm. © Zedcor Wholly Owned/Thinkstock. 22: mr. © George Doyle/Thinkstock, bl. © Garret Bautista/Fotolia, tl. © Iosif Szasz-Fabian/Fotolia, tml. © Anetta/Fotolia, tmr. © Getty Images/Hemera Technologies/Thinkstock, tr. © Kasoga/Fotolia, ml. © James Steidl/Fotolia, mml. © Hemera Technologies/Thinkstock, mmr. © Jiri Hera/Fotolia, br. © TrudiDesign/Fotolia. 23: tl. © Gravicapa/Fotolia, bm. © Hemera Technologies/Thinkstock, mbm. © George Doyle/Thinkstock, tr. © Getty Images/Hemera Technologies/ Thinkstock, bl. © Garret Bautista/Fotolia, tm. © James Steidl/Fotolia, mtl. © Olga Sapegina/Fotolia, mtm. © Iosif Szasz-Fabian/Fotolia, mtr. © Thomas Northcut/Thinkstock, mbl. © Getty Images/ Polka Dot RF/Thinkstock, br. © Ablestock.com/Thinkstock. 24: tl. © Marcel Hurni/Fotolia, mml. © Comstock/Thinkstock, br. © George Doyle/Thinkstock, tml. © Valua Vitaly/Fotolia, tmr. © r-o-x-o-r/Fotolia, tr. © Getty Images/Polka Dot RF/ Thinkstock, ml. © Iosif Szasz-Fabian/Fotolia, mmr. © James Steidl/Fotolia, mr. © Thomas Northcut/Thinkstock, bml. © Hemera Technologies/ Thinkstock, bmr. © Jiri Hera/Fotolia, bl. © auris/Fotolia. 25: tm. © Roger Scott/Fotolia, bm. © Eray/Fotolia, tl. © imrek/Fotolia, tr. © Hemera Technologies/Thinkstock, ml. © James Steidl/Fotolia, m. © Jaimie Duplass/Fotolia, mr. © Lasse Kristensen/Fotolia, bl. © Blueee/Fotolia, br. © Thomas Northcut/Thinkstock, mr. © Sergik/Fotolia. 26: bl. © Yxowert/Fotolia, mbl. © Eray/Fotolia, mbm. © Emilia Stasiak/Fotolia, mtl. © Lilyana Vynogradova/Fotolia, tm. © imrek/Fotolia, tr. © Solodovnikova Elena/Fotolia, ml. © Oleg Shelomentsev/Fotolia, mtr. © Valua Vitaly/Fotolia, mtr. © Jaimie Duplass/Fotolia, bm. © Hemera Technologies/Thinkstock, br. © Lasse Kristensen/Fotolia, mbr. © Elaine Barker/Fotolia. 27: tml. © Yui/ Fotolia, bmr. © Jupiterimages/Thinkstock, bml. © Victoria Liu/Fotolia, tl. © Jupiterimages/Thinkstock, tmr. © Marie-Thérèse GUIHAL/Fotolia, ml. © Nbriam/Fotolia, mmr. © Hemera Technologies/Thinkstock, bl. © Stockbyte/Thinkstock, br. © Lev Olkha/Fotolia, tr. © Iznogood/Fotolia, mml. © Iznogood/Fotolia. 28: br. © Yui/Fotolia, mbr. © Jupiterimages/Thinkstock, tl. © Victoria Liu/Fotolia, bm. © Jupiterimages/Thinkstock, mbl. © Linous/Fotolia, tm. © Solodovnikova Elena/Fotolia, mtl. © Lev Olkha/Fotolia, mtr. © Nbriam/Fotolia, mbm. © Hemera Technologies/Thinkstock, bl. © 0neuser/Fotolia, tr. © Iznogood/Fotolia, mtm. © Iznogood/Fotolia. 29: bl. © Abderit99/Fotolia, tl. © Jstock/Fotolia, tl. © Petr Masek/Fotolia, tm. © Thomas Northcut/Thinkstock, tr. © PhotoObjects.net/Thinkstock, ml. © Ablestock.com/Thinkstock, m. © Hemera Technologies/Thinkstock, mr. © r-o-x-o-r/Fotolia, bm. © Johnny Lye/Fotolia. 30: mbl. © Jstock/Fotolia, mbr. © Petr Masek/Fotolia, br. © Diginatur/Fotolia, bm. © DC Productions/

A B C

D E F

G H I

J K L

c   b   a

f   e   d

i   h   g

l   k   j

M N O

P Q R

S T U

V W X

o n m

r q p

u t s

x w v

Y Z A

B C D

E F G

H I J

a	z	y
d	c	b
g	f	e
j	i	h

K L M

N O P

Q R S

T U V

m l k

p o n

s r q

v u t

W X Y

Z A E

I O U

L S T

y x w

e a z

u o i

t s l

said

Lesson 37, pages 81–82

do

Lesson 45, pages 97–98

you

Lesson 45, pages 97–98

my

Lesson 37, pages 81–82

are

Lesson 45, pages 97–98

like

Lesson 45, pages 97–98

I

Lesson 37, pages 81–82

with

Lesson 37, pages 81–82

for

Lesson 45, pages 97–98

here

Lesson 37, pages 81–82

the

Lesson 37, pages 81–82

down

Lesson 45, pages 97–98

come

Lesson 60, pages 127–128

have

Lesson 60, pages 127–128

her

Lesson 60, pages 127–128

one

Lesson 60, pages 127–128

our

Lesson 60, pages 127–128

out

Lesson 77, pages 163–164

of

Lesson 60, pages 127–128

two

Lesson 77, pages 163–164

were

Lesson 77, pages 163–164

where

Lesson 77, pages 163–164

they

Lesson 77, pages 163–164

your

Lesson 77, pages 163–164

long

Lesson 85, pages 179–180

from

Lesson 103, pages 215–216

which

Lesson 103, pages 215–216

little

Lesson 85, pages 179–180

because

Lesson 103, pages 215–216

want

Lesson 103, pages 215–216

could

Lesson 85, pages 179–180

why

Lesson 85, pages 179–180

them

Lesson 103, pages 215–216

about

Lesson 85, pages 179–180

there

Lesson 85, pages 179–180

their

Lesson 103, pages 215–216

Name

My Cards